CliffsN~~otes~~
Getting Out of Debt

by Cynthia Clampitt

IN THIS BOOK

- Figure out just how far in debt you are
- Put together a budget to get yourself on track
- Improve your debt picture by moving money to put toward your debt
- Stay out of debt for good once you get yourself out
- Reinforce what you learn with the CliffsNotes Review
- Find more information about getting out of debt in the Cliffs-Notes Resource Center and online at www.cliffsnotes.com

IDG Books Worldwide, Inc.
An International Data Group Company
Foster City, CA • Chicago, IL • Indianapolis, IN • New York, NY

IDG BOOKS
WORLDWIDE

About the Author

Cynthia Clampitt is a freelance writer and photographer with a wide range of experience, including writing on economics, business, travel, food and nutrition, history, and literature. She has published articles on financial planning and money management and has written consumer economics materials for two major educational publishers.

Publisher's Acknowledgments

Editorial

Senior Project Editor: Pamela Mourouzis
Senior Acquisitions Editor: Mark Butler
Associate Acquisitions Editor: Karen Hansen
Copy Editor: Patricia Yuu Pan
Technical Editors: David Mylenbusch;
J. Patrick Gorman

Production

IDG Books Indianapolis Production Department
Proofreader: Chris Collins
Indexer: Johnna VanHoose

CliffsNotes™ Getting Out of Debt
Published by
IDG Books Worldwide, Inc.
An International Data Group Company
919 E. Hillsdale Blvd.
Suite 400
Foster City, CA 94404
www.idgbooks.com (IDG Books Worldwide Web site)
www.cliffsnotes.com (Cliffs Notes Web site)

Library of Congress Catalog Card No.: 99-648-69
ISBN: 0-7645-8513-4
Printed in the United States of America
10 9 8 7 6 5 4 3 2 1
1O/RR/QY/ZZ/IN
Distributed in the United States by IDG Books Worldwide, Inc.
Distributed by CDG Books Canada Inc. for Canada; by Transworld Publishers Limited in the United Kingdom; by IDG Norge Books for Norway; by IDG Sweden Books for Sweden; by IDG Books Australia Publishing Corporation Pty. Ltd. for Australia and New Zealand; by TransQuest Publishers Pte Ltd. for Singapore, Malaysia, Thailand, Indonesia, and Hong Kong; by Gotop Information Inc. for Taiwan; by ICG Muse, Inc. for Japan; by Norma Comunicaciones S.A. for Colombia; by Intersoft for South Africa; by Eyrolles for France; by International Thomson Publishing for Germany, Austria and Switzerland; by Distribuidora Cuspide for Argentina; by LR International; by Ediciones ZETA S.C.R. Ltda. for Peru; by WS Computer Publishing Corporation, Inc., for the Philippines; by Contemporanea de Ediciones for Venezuela; by Express Computer Distributors for the Caribbean and West Indies; by Micronesia Media Distributor, Inc. for Micronesia; by Grupo Editorial Norma S.A. for Guatemala; by Chips Computadoras S.A. de C.V. for Mexico; by Editorial Norma de Panama S.A. for Panama; by American Bookshops for Finland. Authorized Sales Agent: Anthony Rudkin Associates for the Middle East and North Africa.
For general information on IDG Books Worldwide's books in the U.S., please call our Consumer Customer Service department at **800-762-2974**. For reseller information, including discounts and premium sales, please call our Reseller Customer Service department at **800-434-3422**.
For information on where to purchase IDG Books Worldwide's books outside the U.S., please contact our International Sales department at 317-596-5530 or fax **317-596-5692**.
For consumer information on foreign language translations, please contact our Customer Service department at **800-434-3422**, fax **317-596-5692**, or e-mail rights@idgbooks.com.
For information on licensing foreign or domestic rights, please phone **650-655-3109**.
For sales inquiries and special prices for bulk quantities, please contact our Sales department at 650-655-3200 or write to the address above.
For information on using IDG Books Worldwide's books in the classroom or for ordering examination copies, please contact our Educational Sales department at **800-434-2086** or fax **317-596-5499**.
For press review copies, author interviews, or other publicity information, please contact our Public Relations department at **650-655-3000** or fax **650-655-3299**.
For authorization to photocopy items for corporate, personal, or educational use, please contact Copyright Clearance Center, 222 Rosewood Drive, Danvers, MA 01923, or fax **978-750-4470**.

IDG BOOKS WORLDWIDE

Table of Contents

INTRODUCTION

Simply stated, debt is the flip side of the credit coin. Someone extended credit to you, and now you have to repay that person or institution.

Whether your debt is simply annoying because it's cutting into your buying power or is overwhelming because it's out of control, you *can* get your finances back where you want them to be. Doing so takes work, discipline, and serious soul-searching, but there's no reason you can't break free of debt's bondage. This book is designed to set you on the right path, give you some of the tools you need, and reassure you that there's light at the end of the tunnel.

In this book, you'll learn how to sort your debt by type, create a budget, and find extra money. You'll also discover ideas and guidelines about changing the patterns that got you into debt in the first place, having fun even when you're broke, and looking forward to building a stable financial future.

Like any advice, the degree to which the recommendations in this book can help depends largely on your situation, your ability to assess your situation realistically, and your willingness to make the effort. Your reward can go beyond simply getting out of debt to staying out for good, and even finding yourself in an enviable financial situation at some point in the foreseeable future. But you have to do the work.

Why wait any longer to free yourself of the panic, headaches, decreased spending power, and limited future that excess debt brings? Get started today!

Why Do You Need This Book?

Can you answer yes to any of these questions?

- Do you need to learn about getting out of debt fast?

- Don't have time to read 500 pages on getting out of debt?

- Have you gone crazy with your credit cards?

- Have unforeseen circumstances run up your bills beyond your ability to pay?

- Do you need a basic book on how to get your bills under control?

Then CliffsNotes *Getting Out of Debt* is for you!

How to Use This Book

This book gives you a lot of guidelines, suggestions, information, ideas, and resources. It includes exercises for you to do and actions for you to take. Not everything applies to you, but do consider all the information carefully, because you don't want to make a quick judgment and toss out something that might have been a key to your financial success.

You decide the best way for you to use this book. What's important is that you use it to help yourself get out of debt — and stay out. Here are some ways that I recommend you search for the information you need:

- Use the index at the back of the book.

- Flip through the book and look for your topic in the running head across the top of each page.

- Check the table of contents at the front of the book.

- Look through the In This Chapter list at the beginning of each chapter.

■ Flip through the book until you find what you need — the book is organized in a logical, task-oriented way.

For additional sources of information about money management, check the CliffsNotes Resource Center at the back of the book.

The following icons, which appear throughout the series, are designed to highlight vital concepts or particularly useful pieces of information throughout the book. They provide an easy way to navigate and focus.

This icon points out information that is too important to forget.

This icon gives you a heads-up on potentially dangerous situations.

This icon highlights words of wisdom that will save you some time and energy and perhaps spare you a headache or two.

After you've read the book, when you need to review the material, these icons can help you return to important points or remind you of key ideas.

Don't Miss Our Web Site

Keep up with the exciting world of personal finance by visiting our Web site at www.cliffsnotes.com. Here's what you find:

■ Interactive tools that are fun and informative

■ Links to interesting Web sites

■ Additional resources to help you continue your learning

At www.cliffsnotes.com, you can even register for a new feature called CliffsNotes Daily, which offers you newsletters on a variety of topics, delivered right to your e-mail inbox each business day.

If you haven't yet discovered the Internet and are wondering how to get online, pick up *Getting On the Internet,* new from CliffsNotes. You learn just what you need to make your online connection quickly and easily. See you at www.cliffsnotes.com!

CHAPTER 1

UNDERSTANDING DEBTS AND EXPENSES

IN THIS CHAPTER

- Defining credit, debt, and expenses
- Looking at secured and unsecured loans
- Pinning down essential, nonessential, and borderline/ debatable expenses
- Categorizing your expenses

Knowing the different types of debts and expenses that drain the money out of your pocket every month can help you prioritize your payments and identify places to cut back. This knowledge also helps you assess how effective your choices are likely to be; some of the available options may or may not help, depending on the type of debt that you have.

Credit

To understand debt and what effect it has on your future, you need to understand credit. This book deals only with personal credit, which has two aspects: having funds put at your disposal (loans, cash advances), and time given for payment of goods and services sold on trust (credit cards, installment plans). Both involve the promise of future repayment, usually with interest.

The way you get credit is by establishing *creditworthiness*, which is a measure of your reliability to repay a loan. Lenders consider three factors in determining creditworthiness:

- **Capacity:** The measure of your ability to repay; refers primarily to your income.

- **Capital:** The value of what you own, including property, investments, and savings.

- **Character:** Generally regarded as the most important factor. To determine your character, lenders rely on reports of your credit history.

Credit bureaus collect information on the borrowing and repayment patterns of all consumers. They put everything about you that might affect repayment — including your employer, income, mortgage, outstanding bills, legal problems, and available credit — into this history. Credit reports that are sent to potential lenders, and often to employers when you apply for jobs, are based on this credit history.

The reason credit histories suffer so badly when you don't pay your bills is that credit is not merely a convenience. It is a legal contract built on a foundation of trust. In failing to pay bills, you are both breaking the law and betraying trust. Most consumers don't think of credit this way, but creditors do. You may want to think about how you view credit, because it affects how you use it.

Debt

Debt is anything owed. Debt can be very short-term, like ordering a meal and having to pay for it before you leave, or long-term, like buying a house with a 30-year mortgage. Whatever you have to pay is a debt.

Chapter 2 provides guidelines to help you determine whether your debt is enough to worry about. However, any debt is too much if you're not completely comfortable with it. If you can't easily pay all your bills every month, or if you carry a balance on any of your credit cards, you're already wading into the bog. If you don't do something to change your direction, you'll be in over your head before you know it.

Debts are broken into a variety of categories, and understanding these categories can help you prioritize your payments. All debts are either secured or unsecured.

Secured loans

A *secured loan* is a loan backed by something of value that you pledge to insure payment. You make a promise, usually in the form of a printed security agreement, stating that the creditor can take a specified item of your property if you fail to pay back the loan.

Often, the item pledged is the one being purchased. The pledged item can also be an item that you already own. If you stop paying for any reason, the pledged item goes to the creditor.

The most common items purchased by a secured loan are

- Houses and condos

- Motor vehicles (cars, trucks, and motorcycles)

- Major appliances, such as refrigerators and washing machines

- Furniture

- Expensive jewelry

Generally speaking, secured loans are high priorities in your debt-repayment plan, especially if the loan is for a home or transportation. You might be willing to have someone repossess a diamond necklace, but you certainly don't want anyone foreclosing on your mortgage and repossessing your home.

Unsecured loans

An *unsecured loan* is a loan not backed by collateral. The majority of debt in the United States is in the form of unsecured loans — primarily credit cards — but this category also includes student loans, personal loans, and medical bills. (Personal loans are unsecured loans that you take out to pay for specific expenditures, such as a vacation, a wedding, or a major appliance.) The lender grants you credit based on your creditworthiness or, in some cases, on the creditworthiness of a cosigner.

Because unsecured loans are riskier for lenders, most of these loans have higher interest rates than secured loans do. Due to the high interest rates, particularly on credit cards, these loans can represent the biggest drain on your finances.

Expenses

Expense is spending or cost — just another form of debt, really. But expense is traditionally short term, like food or the phone bill. (Of course, putting expenses on a credit card makes them part of your "real" debts, with the increased possibility of added interest payments.)

Many sources use the terms *expense* and *debt* interchangeably, so understand that whichever term is used, it always ends up meaning that money is going out.

Essential expenses

Some expenses must be paid, either because of the law or because you still need someplace to live, even if you're broke. These essential expenses are divided into two categories: essential fixed expenses and essential variable expenses.

Essential fixed expenses do not vary from month to month. You may see annual increases in some categories, but you can often anticipate these expenses and plan for them.

Essential fixed expenses include the following:

- Rent or mortgage payments
- Car payments
- Insurance (auto, health, life)
- Alimony/child support

Essential variable expenses differ from month to month, but they often offer you a greater opportunity to cut costs, either by finding less-expensive alternatives or by cutting back on use. Following are examples of essential variable expenses:

- Food
- Utilities (water, gas, electricity)
- Phone
- Gasoline or other transportation costs
- Medical expenses

Other payments are not normally included under essential expenses — primarily debt repayment — because these payments are not considered part of an "ideal" budget. They include payments on secured loans (other than home equity or improvement loans and mortgages), unsecured loans, student loans, personal loans, and installment payment plans.

Remember

Because your goal is to be debt-free and financially independent, you want to keep repaying your debts.

Another essential expense is taxes. Most of the time, adequate taxes are deducted from your paychecks. But if you find at the end of the year that you owe taxes, the expense can add to your debt burden. Of course, if you're self-employed, the expense may become a problem even before the end of the tax year. Either way, you need to keep a few things in mind when you're trying to prioritize your payments:

■ Paying taxes is always and unequivocally essential, if for no other reason than that these guys can hurt you worse than almost anyone else.

■ That said, the Internal Revenue Service (IRS) wants to help you pay your taxes. The IRS offers more than 100 taxpayer information publications, including one on free tax services. Also, the IRS can help you put together a payment schedule for paying your taxes.

■ If you owe back taxes, the IRS will help you plan your budget — but be aware that they will be fairly ruthless in cutting things out of your budget and may not have the same priorities that you have. So it's better to keep the IRS happy by staying current (even if on a payment plan) and creating your own budget.

■ Even if you declare bankruptcy, you still have to pay your taxes. There's no escaping them, so you may as well plan to pay them.

Nonessential expenses

Just about everything that's not listed in the "Essential expenses" section is nonessential. Some services, conveniences, and luxuries have become such a normal part of everyday life that you may think that they're essential, but they're not.

Popular nonessentials include

- Cable TV

- Lawn service

- Cleaning service

- Magazine subscriptions (unless they're business related)

- Cigarettes

- Restaurant meals

- Movies (especially full-priced ones)

- Club memberships

Borderline/Debatable expenses

Just as one person's meat is another person's poison, so, too, one person's nonessential expense can be another person's necessity. Because no one else possesses precisely the same combination of characteristics, needs, priorities, and circumstances that you do, some expenses — perhaps many — require careful consideration. It's important to be honest with yourself about what's really necessary, and not simply something to which you're accustomed.

An expense is considered borderline or debatable when, due to circumstances or life situation, it cannot easily be dropped into either the essential or the nonessential category. Borderline expenses may be nonessential in themselves, but you may be nearly finished paying for something with no hope of regaining your investment. They may be debts owed to people you can talk into waiting a little while longer for repayment.

Following are examples of expenses that may be borderline or debatable:

- **If you're young and healthy, permanent life insurance is debatable.** Consider term life insurance until you're out of debt.

- **Health club membership may be debatable.** If you just signed up and owe thousands, dump the membership. If you paid a huge, nonrefundable initiation fee several years ago and pay only a small monthly or annual maintenance fee now, the membership is probably worth keeping — especially if you use the health club as a low-cost alternative to costlier activities.

- **Health and auto insurance may be essential, but low deductibles aren't.** Find out whether you can lower your payments by having a higher deductible. However, make sure to budget for extra savings to cover the higher deductible.

- **Clothes are less debatable than you may think.** For most people (other than growing children), clothes don't need to be replaced that often. Consider sticking with what you have for a couple of years unless something disintegrates or you have to go on a job interview and you don't own anything appropriate.

Identifying your expense types

Now you know how to divide expenses and debts. The next step is to identify how your expenses and debts can be categorized.

On a piece of paper, write down everything on which you spend money. Include as much detail as possible in your list, making the list as long as necessary.

Although big purchases obviously cause greater debt, the little, unplanned things — the ones you hardly even notice — are often the ones that undercut your best intentions. For example, snacking out of vending machines combined with stopping for gourmet coffee on the way to work each day can add up to nearly $1,000 a year.

Using the following codes, identify the status of each expense item on your list:

- S = Secured loan
- U = Unsecured loan
- EF = Essential fixed expense
- EV = Essential variable expense
- N = Nonessential expense
- R = Expense that can be reduced
- C = Expense that can be cut entirely
- ? = Need to research whether this expense can be reduced or cut

Note: You don't see a code for borderline/debatable items because items are borderline only until you decide which category they belong in. Making that decision is one of the things you need to accomplish in this exercise.

The following sample gives you an idea of how your worksheet might look.

Items on Which I Spend Money

Mortgage	S, EF, ?
Food	EV, R
Phone, general	EV, R
Phone, extras	_____

Entertainment	_____
Magazines	_____
Gasoline	_____
Health club	_____
Beverages purchased at office	_____
Car payment	_____
Life insurance	_____
Personal loan	_____
Cable TV	_____

Continue to add lines, making the list as long as necessary. You want to account for everything on which you spend money.

This chart is not a contract. Expenses do not need to remain static. As circumstances change, you can add or delete items or change the status of an item. If a job change makes it necessary for you to have a pager, for example, you can simply move that expense from the nonessential to the essential category.

For the next few days, you may want to keep a notebook and jot down items that you didn't think to add to this list. (Those items could include the toll you always pay on the way to work, the laundry money you always toss in a jar so that you'll have it when you need it, or the drink that you have with friends every Friday night.) The more aware you are of where your money goes, the easier it is to keep your expenses under control.

By the time you're through with this worksheet, you should have a pretty good idea of where your money is going, what you must include in your budget, and where you can cut back.

Remember

You can reduce most expenses if you put your mind to it. The more you reduce expenses, the more quickly you can improve your financial situation and get started down the path to financial freedom and creditworthiness.

CHAPTER 2

ASSESSING YOUR SITUATION

IN THIS CHAPTER

- Gathering the tools you need to get started
- Figuring out how much you owe
- Determining how you got into debt
- Setting your priorities
- Looking at the resources you have for solving the problem

One thing that's true for everyone is that, in order to plan how to get somewhere, you have to know where you're starting. That's why you need to start by assessing your financial situation.

How you got into debt is particularly significant because the work you need to do and the changes you want to make will be different if, for example, your debts were caused by a job loss as opposed to uncontrolled spending. Determining your priorities will help you later in the budgeting and rebuilding process.

Preparing Your Work Area and Gathering Your Tools

Your first step is to prepare your workspace. Clear an area in which you can work without having to move things for a while (in other words, a table that you don't need to clear off for meals or for doing other work). This project might take a bit of time, and if you need to get back to it later, you don't want to get slowed down or possibly sidetracked by having to put everything away.

You want your work area to be someplace you'll see it regularly so you'll be reminded that you should be making progress. However, you don't need to set up your work area where visiting neighbors are likely to see it. This is not an exercise in humiliation, just a way of making it difficult to forget.

After you identify your work area, gather the following items:

- Pens, pencils, erasers, and pencil sharpener

- Pads of lined paper and lots of scratch paper

- Calculator

- All outstanding bills, loan vouchers, and statements of any kind (including mortgage, student loans, and anything else that you owe)

- Paycheck stubs

- Information about other sources of income (interest payments, child support, royalties, and so on)

- Information about assets, savings, and property

As you progress, you may find that you need or want more equipment, such as a computer and financial software. You can easily work these items into the process, but you don't need them at the beginning. In fact, if you don't have a computer, you can handle this entire process with pencil and paper — so don't think that you need to run out and invest in an array of computer hardware and gadgets and put yourself further into debt!

Finally, set aside time to work on this project. If you wait to "find" time, you'll end up doing nothing. You must determine to create the space in your schedule, because your financial future depends on it.

Consider setting aside an entire morning or afternoon to get started. You may need to get back to it for another hour or two at a later time, until you have a good plan worked out. After that, an hour or so each week can go toward the reviewing, learning, and ongoing planning that are necessary to make you financially solid.

Financial planning is a process. It is never really "over," because you'll use money your whole life. The process takes time, but it's worth the effort. And like any "exercise," it gets easier as you get stronger and in better "shape."

Figuring Out How Much You Owe

You can set your repayment priorities later. Right now, you need to figure out how far in debt you really are.

Total debt

It's time to pick up a pencil and paper and grab your calculator.

Use the following worksheet as an example to record all your debts. Total up your debts by type, and then calculate your grand total. This final number represents your total outstanding debt. If an item in the example worksheet doesn't apply to you, skip it; also feel free to add or delete items so that the worksheet accurately reflects your debt.

Home

Mortgage	$_____
Home equity loan	$_____
Furniture on installment plan	$_____
Appliances on installment plan	$_____
Past-due utility bills	$_____
Total Home Debt	*$_____*

Auto

Loan, car 1	$_____
Loan, car 2	$_____
Total Auto Debt	*$_____*

Credit Cards

MasterCard	$_____
Visa	$_____
Discover	$_____
Other	$_____
Total Credit Card Debt	*$_____*

Miscellaneous

Medical bills	$_____
Personal loans	$_____
Student loans	$_____
Other loans	$_____
Total Miscellaneous Debt	*$_____*

Outstanding Taxes

Federal	$_____
State	$_____
Other	$_____
Total Tax Debt	*$_____*
Total All Debts	**$_____**

Notice that I didn't have you include regular expenses like utilities (unless they're past due), food, and fuel. That's because, even though these expenses arise regularly, they really aren't part of your debt (unless you charge them). However, they do have an impact on how much money is available to go toward your debts. So don't get rid of any information that you have on these expenses, because you'll need it when you do your budget. (See Chapter 4.)

Rent and lease payments were also excluded, because they are not debt in the same sense that a loan is, although you are legally obligated to pay both, even if you give up the apartment or car. Also, alimony and child support were not included. Although these are all debt obligations, if you owe them, and have to be part of your calculations, they are not things that you can pay off early or reduce.

You need to do one more thing while you have your bills handy: Write the interest rate being charged for each credit card and loan next to the amount due. This information will be helpful later.

Debt as percentage of income

To determine how serious your debt is, you need to determine how much of your monthly net income (that's income after taxes — your actual take-home pay) is going toward paying debt. To do so, follow these steps:

1. Add up your *monthly* debt obligations, including rent or mortgage payment, auto lease or loan payments, other loan payments, credit card payments, alimony, and child support.

2. Divide the total by the amount of your monthly income after taxes.

For example, imagine that you have a mortgage payment of $800, an auto loan payment of $300, a credit card payment of $100, a student loan payment of $200, an installment loan payment of $100, and take-home pay of $4,500. Here's how this monthly debt obligation translates into debt as percentage of income:

$800 + $300 + $100 + $200 + $100 = $1,500 in monthly debt obligations

$1,500 ÷ $4,500 = 33.3 percent

In other words, 33.3 percent of your monthly net income ($4,500) goes toward paying off debt.

If your debt obligations are 25 percent or less of your take-home pay, you're in good shape. If they're between 25 and 35 percent, you should be concerned and begin thinking about how you can try to get closer to 25 percent. If they're over 35 percent, you're headed for serious trouble or may already be there — you must move quickly to reduce debt.

The 33.3 percent in the sample formula, therefore, is not yet catastrophic but is well into the "time to get serious about debt" range.

On a card or piece of note paper, write your current percentage, and then write next to it the percentage to aim for (25 percent or less). Write today's date on the card, and write down how long you think it will take you to achieve your goals. (Don't worry, you can always revise this estimate as you progress.) Place it somewhere you can see it regularly to help you keep your goal in mind.

Looking at How You Got into Debt

It's possible that you played no part in the accumulation of debt — you may have inherited it from others or acquired it as a result of circumstances beyond your control, such as a serious illness or a natural disaster. In that case, you simply need to address the mechanics of paying bills and rebuilding credit. With a few money-saving and debt-retiring strategies, you may find yourself in a stronger position than before your debts accrued.

Most people, however, have a pattern of debt — a series of behaviors that get them into the hole. The more uncertain you are of how you got into trouble, the more likely it is that you'll need to change some of your behaviors.

This exercise helps you determine how you got into debt. You need to be really honest with yourself for this to work. If you've run up thousands of dollars in credit card debt, don't call it "bad luck." Get a sheet of paper and start to write down behaviors or triggers that get you into trouble. Don't judge yourself or your debts as you write. Simply write down everything that's fueling your debt.

To get started on your list, ask yourself the following questions:

- Why did I take on my first debt?

- How do I feel about debt?

- How does spending money make me feel?

- Do I ever "binge shop"? If so, what sorts of things trigger the binges?

- What reaction do I have to advertisements for items that I want but can't afford?

- Do I believe that paying the minimum amount on my credit card will get the balance paid off?

- Am I ever surprised by how high a bill is?

- Do I forget about money that I've spent?

- Do I balance my checking account regularly?

- Do I have any expensive hobbies or habits?

- Do I feel competitive with or threatened by those around me?

- How often do I eat out?

- When I eat out, do I collect cash from others and charge the meal?

- Do I plan my purchases, or do I buy on impulse?

Review your list on how much you owe. The information may give you even more ideas about how you got into debt. Add any discoveries to your list of trouble behaviors and triggers.

As you write, more ideas may come to you. Record everything that crosses your mind regarding your spending habits, whether it's a feeling that you must pamper yourself to deal with stress, a hope that you can overcome your sense of dissatisfaction with life, or a belief that you need to impress someone.

A journal can be particularly helpful in identifying emotion-triggered spending, as well as in tracking your progress and recording what you learn, both about the process and about yourself.

As you continue through the rest of this book, add to your list any new information that you discover about yourself. Knowing why you spend and what your triggers are can help you figure out how to stop uncontrolled spending.

Determining Your Priorities

Obviously, one major priority is to get out of debt. At this point, however, you need to think about what your priorities in life are, how they relate to or might be affected by debt, and how they fit into the process of getting out of debt.

For this exercise, think about your *real* priorities — the things that matter deeply to you. You need to account for considerations like family and beliefs first and foremost, no matter what type of debt you're facing.

Later, when you start to create your budget, you can prioritize your "wish list" — the things that you would like but that aren't really vital in the greater scheme of things — in order to identify expenses that you can reduce or cut. But right now, think about the priorities that will help you determine what kind of path you will take.

Here are some questions to ask yourself as you think about your priorities:

- Where does my family fit into the picture? (For example, do we have financial obligations, such as a child's college tuition, that we have to account for?)

- Is taking a second job an option (financially, emotionally)?

- Is giving to charity or religious organizations important to me?

- For my own peace of mind, how quickly do I want to be out of debt? What am I willing to sacrifice to get there?

- What things that are important to me are affected by my debt, or might be affected by it if I do not remedy it? (These might include anything from not being able to join friends for dinner to having to postpone starting a family or losing your house.)

- What goals do I have that might be attainable once I'm out of debt? (These could be anything from educating children to a comfortable retirement.)

As you think about your priorities, jot down the things that matter most to you — the things that have an impact on how and why you want to get out of debt.

If you have young children or aging parents, you may not view a second job as an option. In this case, you're making family a priority and accepting the possibility of a slightly longer repayment period. The debts aren't going anywhere, but the people are, so this is a good choice. Getting out of debt is about making your life better, not worse.

Looking at Your Resources and Assets

In evaluating the resources and assets you have for getting yourself out of debt, consider not only your income but also any capital available, including savings, investments, and property. This exercise has two steps:

1. Calculate your monthly income. You'll use this figure later to work out your budget. Because income can change over time, the wisest approach is simply to figure out what you're taking in at the present time.

2. Determine any additional funds that may be available to you. If you need to make dramatic changes in your debt profile, also consider potential sources of money.

Set up your calculations as in the following worksheet, with the various real or potential sources of funds separated.

Income (After Taxes)

Primary wages	$_____	
Secondary wages (second job/ secondary wage earner)	$_____	
Alimony/Child support	$_____	
Other income	$_____	
Total Income		*$_____*

Easily Accessible Money

Savings	$_____
Investments	$_____
Total Easily Accessible Money	*$_____*

Less-Accessible Money

Home equity	$_____
Car equity	$_____
Boat equity	$_____
Other (such as equity in a vacation home or undeveloped property)	$_____
Cash-value insurance	$_____
Total Less-Accessible Money	*$_____*

Other Possible (Though Less Desirable) Sources of Money

IRAs	$_____
401(k)	$_____
Total Other Sources of Money	*$_____*

Reviewing your assets helps you determine where your money is, which, in turn, helps you with both the budgeting process (see Chapter 3) and improving your debt picture (see Chapters 4 and 5).

CHAPTER 3
PUTTING TOGETHER A BUDGET

IN THIS CHAPTER

- Determining your goals for paying down your debts
- Creating a budget
- Evaluating and staying up-to-date with your budget

In Chapter 2, you determined where you are in terms of your debt — your starting point. You also began to think about where you're going. Now it's time to plan the "trip." This process includes setting specific goals, determining how long the journey should take, and creating a "map" to help you get there.

This map is your budget, which helps you do two things: plan your spending and track your progress. A budget may seem restrictive at first, but it frees you from the worry of not knowing how you're doing financially. A budget can give you greater control and keep you on the road to your destination: freedom from debt.

Determining and Refining Your Debt-Repayment Goals

Setting goals takes effort. You need to think carefully about where you want to be financially, as well as what future plans you have that might be affected by your finances. You also need to be reasonable and not set impossible goals for yourself. Take this process seriously, but don't panic about it — you can modify your goals as time goes by.

The following are the key elements that you need to consider to create goals that are both attainable and motivating.

Be positive

You don't want "spend less money" as a goal because it's negative, and staying motivated by a negative goal is difficult. Charting your progress is also difficult — how do you determine when you are spending enough less?

Instead, your goal should be something like "enjoy the freedom of carrying a debt load of only 25 percent of my take-home pay." That goal is positive and quantifiable. Other possibilities might be "pick up the mail without being nervous," "feel that I am in control of my finances," or "get to a point where I can start investing so that more money is coming in than going out." These goals aren't as easily quantifiable as the percentage-of-take-home-pay goal, but the point is to find something that keeps you motivated and excited about the process.

To be effective, your goal needs to be in the form of an accomplishment, not a sacrifice.

Take your plans into account

In a way, you've already established one goal: to be out of debt. Although this is your primary goal, you may want to consider other, secondary goals, which will be made possible by your success with your primary goal.

Depending on where you are in life, your plans may be to have children, put children through college, buy a house, or have a secure retirement. All these goals will benefit — and some are only possible — if you get your finances under control. The nearer in time your plans lie, the more quickly you want to eliminate your debt and begin saving. For example, if you want to buy a house in five years, you may be willing to work harder to pay off your credit cards so that you can get a mortgage. And you may even want to give yourself an extra year or two to save up for furniture so that you don't get into too much debt again.

Remember

Over time, your lifestyle, earning power, and attitudes may change, so review your goals regularly to make sure that they still reflect your plans.

Establish a time frame

The general structure of goal setting is to establish immediate goals, intermediate goals, and long-term goals.

- **Immediate goals** are goals that you expect to accomplish in the next few weeks, such as finishing your budget, getting started on paying debts, and making necessary adjustments to your spending.

- **Intermediate goals** need to be set at regular intervals — every six months, for example. At these intervals, you can review your accomplishments and reassess your direction. But, as always, there should also be a specific goal, such as "Pay off credit card X by this date."

- **Long-term goals** are the ones that take you to the end of your debt problems and beyond. These goals might include getting to a point where you have no credit card debt, followed by having your debt in the 25 percent range, possibly followed by paying off your mortgage and/or building future wealth.

You can always adjust the dates if you don't accomplish everything you planned by a given date — or if you're paying off debts faster than you expected. These time goals aren't carved in stone, but rather are goalposts — you try to get the ball between the posts, but it doesn't always happen. However, without goalposts, you'll never know whether you scored.

Make sure to allow yourself a realistic amount of time. You probably didn't get into debt overnight, and you certainly won't get out of debt overnight. Generally speaking, you'll probably need at least as much time for getting out of the hole as it took for you to get into it.

So if you went to college for four years by using student loans, then got out and bought a car, and then got a job and started spending money, you probably have put five or six years into accumulating debt. Figure five or six years to become debt-free. Different factors can contribute to getting out of debt in more time or less, including your level of income and your level of commitment to the process.

Think back to when you started to build up your current debt profile. How long ago was it? Look at a calendar and determine a date that is about that far in the future. That date is your long-term goal for being debt-free. You can set short-term and mid-term goals as well, both to help you chart your progress and to help keep you motivated.

Remember, though, that achieving freedom from debt involves sacrifices. You must remain committed to paying back what you owe.

Write down your goals

There are plenty of good reasons for writing down anything that's important:

- You tend to remember information better if you take the time to write it down.

- You're more likely to believe something that you see written out. Seeing it on paper makes it real and tangible.

- You have something to look at, which makes it harder to forget or ignore that you've made a decision.

■ You have proof that you've already accomplished an important task. Goal setting is a major step in the process of getting out of debt, and once you've set the goal, you can start getting excited about the destination.

Write out your positive, long-term goal statement at the top of a sheet of paper. Beneath it, write out the dates you've set for attaining your short-term, mid-term, and long-term goals.

If you haven't already started a file or three-ring binder for the project of getting out of debt, now is a good time to do so. Place your sheet of written goals in the front of the binder or file. This way, you have everything you need in one place: goals, worksheets, and any other information you collect.

In addition to the sheet of paper listing your goals that you put in your file or binder, you can write out your positive, long-term goal statement on a 3 x 5 card and post it where you'll see it regularly, such as on a bathroom mirror.

For your reminder note, you can rephrase the statement in a less formal way. For example, instead of "In five years, I want to have my debt to 25 percent of my take-home pay," you might write it as "If I stick with this, I can be *free* in five years!" Write whatever gets you the most excited about this process. You can then rewrite the note every time you reach an intermediate goal ("Just four more years!"). Updating your note helps keep you out of the "Are we there yet?" syndrome that accompanies many long-term projects.

Creating a Budget

Now it's time to create your plan — your "road map" for getting out of debt. In other words, you're going to create a budget.

There's no perfect form that fits everyone's needs and circumstances, but you do need to consider some basic elements if your budget is going to work. An effective budget needs to be

- **Realistic:** Forcing numbers to work out on paper isn't hard, but these numbers need to work in real life.

Even if you need to watch every penny at this point, don't make the numbers so low that you have no hope of succeeding. If, as you go along, you find ways of cutting costs further, you can always change an entry.

- **Concise yet comprehensive:** You don't want your budget to have so much detail that you spend your whole life keeping it updated, but you do want to include all the expenses that you can identify or predict.

You often can group several expenses into one category. Although you may need to track expenses more precisely from day to day (you may even want to carry a notebook), you can consolidate some items in the budget. (For example, coffee from the gourmet shop, candy from the office vending machine, and a quart of milk on the way home can all be part of the food budget.)

- **Flexible:** Feel free to improve the format of the budget as you continue to work with it. Add more lines if necessary, or delete lines. Change your spending estimates as needed, too. You may find that you guessed too low, or you may discover ways to save money that enable you to lower an amount.

If your financial situation changes — you get married, get a new job, relocate, or have a new mouth to feed — draw up a new budget.

- **Open to all concerned, garnering everyone's cooperation and commitment:** Anyone in the household who contributes to income and/or expenditures needs to be involved in the budget discussions. In particular, those who contribute to the household income need to be in on the planning stages, budget creation, and review process. They need to buy in to the project for it to work.

Small children may not need to be included in the planning, but they should know that something is happening, because the budget will affect them, too. If they feel that they're part of the project, they may be more understanding when you can't buy things for them. In fact, small children may want to contribute by saving their allowance, collecting newspapers or cans, or finding other ways to contribute to the family's success.

To establish your budget, you first want to create a master of the budget worksheet (see Table 3-1) with no numbers filled in. You may want to include a few blank lines in each category on the master, in case you need to add other items later. Then photocopy this master document to create budget worksheets to work on.

A dozen copies (one for each month) is a good start, because you want to work within a budget for at least a year. Even if you can get yourself to that magic 25 percent figure in less time, you should live on a budget for a year to help create a budget mindset that keeps you from falling back into the hole that you just climbed out of. Some people live on a budget their entire lives because it's the only way they can keep themselves out of trouble. You may not have to do so, but if it helps, it's an option.

Your worksheet needs to be well organized and easy to read and keep updated. If working with the budget and calculating totals becomes difficult, you'll give up. This process is serious, so make the effort to create a document that's easy to work with.

Although you'll personalize this worksheet to meet your own needs, some categories need to be a part of everyone's budget. Also, some organizational options may make the budget easier for you to manage. Be sure to do the following:

- Include a space after each item for *estimated expense, actual expense,* and the *difference* between estimated and actual.

- Divide the budget worksheet into *essential* and *nonessential expenses.* You may wish to further divide essential expenses into *fixed* and *variable;* doing so makes it easier to see where you may need to make changes to the budget or to your spending. (The "debt and expense categorization chart" that you created at the end of Chapter 1 can help you accomplish this task.)

- After the total for the expense section, list your sources of *income* and total them.

- The final entry on the budget is the calculation of money remaining. You subtract your total expenses from your total income to determine what remains. The remainder is called your *discretionary income.*

Table 3-1 gives you an idea of what your budget might look like. Feel free to alter the format to meet your own needs, but be sure to include enough information to make the budget effective. And don't forget any debatable items that might not be listed. Also, if you have regular legal or accounting expenses, don't forget to include them.

Table 3-1: Budget Worksheet for (Month) _____

Expense	Estimated	Actual	Difference
Essential Fixed Expenses			
Rent/mortgage	$	$	$
Association fees	$	$	$

Continued

Table 3-1: Budget Worksheet for (Month) _____
(continued)

Expense	Estimated	Actual	Difference
Essential Fixed Expenses			
Car payment	$	$	$
Car insurance	$	$	$
Health insurance	$	$	$
Life insurance	$	$	$
Homeowner's/Renter's insurance	$	$	$
Property taxes	$	$	$
Alimony/child support	$	$	$
_____	$	$	$
Essential Variable Expenses			
Home maintenance	$	$	$
Food	$	$	$
Electricity	$	$	$
Gas (utility)	$	$	$
Water	$	$	$
Phone	$	$	$
Gasoline (auto)	$	$	$
Auto maintenance/repairs	$	$	$
Public transportation	$	$	$
Medical expenses	$	$	$
Childcare	$	$	$
Charitable giving	$	$	$
Household goods (cleaning supplies, cooking utensils, etc.	$	$	$
Savings	$	$	$
_____	$	$	$

Expense	Estimated	Actual	Difference
Fixed Loan Payments			
Student loan	$	$	$
Personal loan	$	$	$
Installment loan 1	$	$	$
Installment loan 2	$	$	$
_____	$	$	$
Credit Card Payments			
MasterCard #1	$	$	$
MasterCard #2	$	$	$
Visa #1	$	$	$
Visa #2	$	$	$
Discover	$	$	$
American Express Optima	$	$	$
Department store card(s)	$	$	$
Gasoline card(s)	$	$	$
Other cards	$	$	$
Charge Cards (Cards That Must Be Paid Off Each Month)			
American Express (regular)	$	$	$
Diner's Club	$	$	$
Nonessential Expenses			
Barber/beautician	$	$	$
Magazine/Newspaper subscriptions	$	$	$
Gifts	$	$	$
Cable TV	$	$	$
Club dues	$	$	$

Continued

Table 3-1: Budget Worksheet for (Month) _____ (continued)

Expense	Estimated	Actual	Difference
Lessons/Camp	$	$	$
Dining out	$	$	$
Movies	$	$	$
Hobbies	$	$	$
Cigarettes	$	$	$
Alcoholic beverages	$	$	$
Domestic help	$	$	$
Lawn service	$	$	$
_____	$	$	$
Total Monthly Expenses	**$**	**$**	**$**
Monthly Income			
Take-home pay (after taxes)	$	$	$
Interest income	$	$	$
Alimony/child support paid to you	$	$	$
_____	$	$	$
Total Monthly Income	*$*	*$*	*$*

Total Money Remaining

Total Monthly Income	$
Total Monthly Expenses	– $
Total Money Remaining	**= $**

Notice that on the sample budget, no blank lines appear under the loan and credit card categories. The simple reason is that you should not be adding items to these categories. If all goes as planned, you'll be eliminating debt categories, not adding them.

You can use the blank lines under the other expense or income categories for seasonal expenses or annual bills, such as auto licenses, vacations, holiday gift purchases, bonuses, and tax preparation services.

If you're self-employed, don't forget to list estimated quarterly taxes under Essential Fixed Expenses.

After you create your own budget worksheet and make copies of the blank form, plug in figures. You'll know some numbers immediately, especially the fixed expenses. (The worksheets that you created in Chapter 2, recording your income and assets and where you spend your money, can help you prepare your budget.) Be as accurate and realistic as possible when filling in amounts.

For utility prices, you can phone your local utility companies. They often can tell you precisely what your average monthly costs have been. Utility companies may also offer a payment plan where you pay the average of your annual bills every month rather than dealing with seasonal dips and rises. Averaged payments can make the budgeting process much easier.

All these figures go in the Estimated column, because you're predicting what your costs will be or what you think you'll be able to put toward paying off your debts. (***Note:*** For fixed essential expenses, for most of the year, the Estimated column will match the Actual column, but the Estimated and Acutal are still included, because they make it easier to total the columns.) Work in pencil so that you can erase entries if necessary. Put down the minimum payment amounts for all credit cards, unless you regularly set and pay a higher amount.

Finally, with all the items in the Estimated column filled in, total your expenses and income, and then figure how much money remains.

Evaluating Your Budget

If your Total Money Remaining figure is zero or negative, you have to revise your budget. First, examine your nonessential expenses. Which ones can be reduced? Which ones can be eliminated? Keep working until you can't think of anything else to reduce. Be honest with yourself about what you can and can't give up or reduce. You really don't need a $65 haircut or cable TV, for example. To succeed, however, don't focus on what you're giving up; focus on what you're gaining: eventual economic freedom.

If you do have money remaining, you can use it to help get yourself out of debt faster, as Chapter 4 explains. If cutting or reducing nonessentials isn't enough to get you into a positive situation, you may need to start examining your essential expenses. Head to Chapter 5 to see how to "find" more money in your budget.

Planning to Stay Up-to-Date

Setting up your budget is just the beginning of your move to financial freedom. Keeping your budget going takes less work than setting it up, but it requires more commitment.

As the month progresses and bills come in, fill in the Actual column for each item and calculate the difference between the estimated amount and the actual amount, noting whether the difference is positive or negative.

Set aside time every month to total the preceding month's worksheet and to review (and update if necessary) your budget for the coming month. You can make seasonal adjustments in order to anticipate times when spending may be higher, or fine-tune entries as you get better at living according to a budget.

The keys to staying up-to-date are

■ **Regularity:** Only by being systematic and updating your records regularly can you get a good picture of your spending patterns. Being consistent helps you know where your money is going and how you're progressing. Also, if you fall behind, catching up may appear to be a discouragingly difficult task.

■ **Accuracy:** You don't have to worry about every penny, but try to be as accurate as possible in recording amounts. Carrying a notebook can help, because you may not remember the vending machine, coffee cart, or newspaper kiosk — the types of expenses that can add $2 or $3 to each day's expense total.

■ **Honesty:** If you're anything less than honest when figuring your budget, you're only hurting yourself. If you record less than what you spend, not only will you never have accurate records, but you may never succeed in getting out of debt. Knowing your true financial picture is the only way to make a budget work.

CHAPTER 4

USING YOUR BUDGET TO GET AHEAD OF YOUR DEBT

IN THIS CHAPTER

- Keeping up with your minimum payments
- Reducing your high-interest debts
- Paying down other debts

When you have a budget in hand, along with a picture of your debt situation, you can strategize about how best to tackle your debt. This chapter tells you how to get started, giving you strategies for reducing your debt. Of course, the primary tool for paying down debt is still the budget — just paying your bills, including your debts, month after month, without adding to your debt burden. But in this chapter, you'll learn how to eliminate the debts that represent the biggest drain on your future buying power.

Using Your Discretionary Income to Pay Off High-Interest Debts First

Discretionary income is the money you have left after you've paid all the bills that you have to pay — the Total Money Remaining figure at the end of your budget worksheet (see Chapter 3). This money is the income that you use at your discretion for "extras," from treats to investing — unless you're in debt.

The budget that you created in Chapter 3 includes items that might normally fall into the discretionary income category (movies, dining out, and so on) simply because at this stage, you have to plan all your expenses. Depending on your level of debt, you may not have much discretionary income after all the items on your budget are accounted for. If you do have some money to spare, you can use it to help get yourself out of debt faster. This process helps cut down on one of the worst drains of money there is: interest payments.

The single most devastating expense you have is the interest on credit cards. Most people don't realize how much they pay in interest or how much difference even the smallest changes can make. Here's an example:

> Say you have a credit card that has a balance of $1,500. If the annual interest is 21 percent (a fairly standard rate) and you make the minimum payment of 3 percent of the balance each month, repaying the total will take you more than 14 years, and you will have paid more than $1,800 in interest (for a total of $3,300).

> If, on that same $1,500, you pay just $5 over the minimum payment each month, you'll save more than $600 on interest and cut more than five years off the repayment time. If you pay $10 more each month, you'll cut nearly $900 and eight years off the interest and time.

These numbers highlight the dramatic difference that even a slight increase in monthly payments can make. But remember that these figures are based on the assumption that you don't spend any more after you run up the initial $1,500. If you keep adding purchases, they all figure into the interest rate, increasing interest payments and making the repayment time longer.

For many reasons — to avoid costly penalties, to maintain a good credit record, to diminish your debt, to keep your creditors at bay — you must continue to make the minimum payment due on each card on which you owe. After you account for those expenses, any discretionary income that you have left in your budget (the amount in the Total Money Remaining column back in Table 3-1) should go toward paying off the credit cards that have the highest interest rates.

If you planned your budget with more than the minimum payment going to each card with an outstanding balance, redo it so that you're paying the minimum on the cards with lower interest rates and putting the rest of your "extra" money toward paying off the highest-interest cards. Follow these steps:

1. After you create your budget and plug in the minimum payment for each credit card, take as much of your discretionary income as possible and use it to pay down the credit card charging the highest interest.

If you wrote the interest rates on your debt worksheet in Chapter 2, you'll be able to tell at a glance which credit card you need to target.

2. After you've paid off the credit card with the highest rate, put your discretionary income toward the credit card with the next highest rate.

3. Continue this process until you've paid off all your credit cards, continuing to take the card with the highest interest rate and put as much discretionary income as possible toward that debt.

Discretionary income is, as its name implies, money that you can use at your discretion. Occasionally, you may want to reserve a little more discretionary income to celebrate the holidays or enjoy a much-needed weekend away. However, until you're getting cozy with that 25 percent debt figure, you want to plow as much of your discretionary income as possible into paying off high-interest debts.

Think of paying off high-interest debts as steps toward improving your future buying power. Nothing eats into your financial potential like a high interest rate.

Cut up your credit cards

Here comes the hard part: As soon as you've paid off the balance on a credit card, cut up the card, mail it back to the bank or other organization that issued it, and close the account.

You may not be able to take the scissors to every credit card you have (because it's nearly impossible to transact business these days without at least one major credit card), but do so with the majority of your cards. Plan to keep one each of the major cards (be sure to pick the ones that have the lowest interest rates, or perhaps ones that require monthly repayment, such as American Express) and get rid of everything else.

In fact, you probably should cut up all but the chosen few cards as soon as you start working on eliminating your debt. (Cutting up a card doesn't mean that you erase the balance, of course, but it does prevent you from making additional purchases on the card.) Whatever you do, don't charge anything while you're still carrying a balance; doing so just makes the interest worse and the repayment time longer. And don't forget to mail it back to the issuer, along with instructions that they close your account — because the account can't be closed until they have the card in hand and know that you won't be using it anymore.

If you must have a charge card (which is possible if you have children, need a card for emergencies, or travel for business), consider getting a new card with no balance. Use this card *only* when you can't use cash or a check, and charge only an amount that you can pay off *completely* when the bill arrives. Because your goal is never again to carry a balance on a credit card, you absolutely do not want to start running up another balance.

Forget your savings for the time being

While you're seriously in debt is the only time in your life that anyone will tell you that your nest egg is a bad idea. If you have any money in a savings account, close the account and put the money toward paying off your high-interest credit cards. Why earn 4 or 5 percent interest on a savings account when you're paying 18 to 21 percent interest on your credit cards?

Liquidate any other assets you have, such as certificates of deposit, stocks, bonds, mutual funds, and even collectibles, and use that money to pay down your high-interest debts as well. Nothing can earn you enough to make it worth keeping in the face of debt on a credit card that charges a 21 percent interest rate.

There are only two exceptions to the "throw everything at your credit cards" plan:

■ Hang onto enough money to cover one month's expenses (if possible), because emergencies do arise. If you can't scrape together a full month's worth, at least save enough to buy food and gas.

■ As long as you can still make the minimum payments on all your debts, don't cash in your retirement funds — 401(k)s, IRAs, and the like. The tax hit and penalties would probably be worse than the interest on your credit cards. Also, jeopardizing your future simply to avoid interest payments is not a good tradeoff.

If you're facing foreclosure, however, that's another matter. Go ahead and liquidate all your assets, including retirement accounts; you don't want to lose your home.

Paying Down Other Debts

If you stick to your budget, you *will* free yourself of credit card debt. That's the good news. The even better news is that your other debts, such as auto loans, student loans, and a mortgage, will also be shrinking as you stick to your budget.

Some types of loans, such as mortgages, assess a prepayment penalty if you pay off the loan early. Make sure to read the fine print on your loan agreement before you end up costing yourself more than you're saving!

If any debts remain after you pay off your credit cards, decide what your next-costliest debts are (perhaps a car payment or an installment loan for a large appliance). Your best bet after paying off credit cards is probably to pay off items that can be repossessed. Simply follow the same procedure for these debts as for the high-interest credit card debts, described earlier in this chapter: Continue to choose the debt with the highest interest and put as much of your discretionary income as possible toward that debt. As you pay off debts, remember to update your budget and reallocate your resources.

Even if you're close to that 25 percent debt figure, you may want to get your ratio of debt to income even lower. Just stick to your budget, don't add to your debt, and you can reach your goals.

CHAPTER 5

MOVING MONEY TO IMPROVE YOUR DEBT PICTURE

IN THIS CHAPTER

- Switching from high-interest to low-interest debts
- Determining whether a home equity loan is for you
- Looking at ways to find more money in your budget

One thing you can do to get a slightly faster start along the path to your final goal of being debt-free is to move your money to where it can do the most good. This tactic includes everything from finding ways to lower your interest payments to locating and plugging the "leaks" in your budget that let money get away from you. This chapter shows you how to do all that and more.

Finding Cheaper Debt

In addition to paying off your high-interest debts (see Chapter 4 for more information about this important debt-reduction strategy), you may also be able to find lower-interest debts to help you get out of debt faster. The following are some sources of cheaper debt.

Lower-interest credit cards

How often do you get offers for credit cards with really low interest rates? Probably almost daily. If you've never taken advantage of these low rates (or you took advantage of them and just ran up more debt), it may be time for you to look at these offers again. Use the form supplied with the offer to transfer balances to the lower-interest account.

Of course, these reduced rates are usually for a limited time only (usually around six months — if it's too short a time, look for a better offer), so check the offer to make sure that the post-hot-deal interest rate isn't higher than what you're paying now. But if the rate after the introductory offer is the same or lower than what you're currently paying, you'll come out ahead even if you can't pay off the whole thing during the trial period.

In addition, some credit cards have a regular interest rate that's lower than the rate on the majority of cards. If you don't have a brochure for a great deal on a new credit card, you can research some of the better rates available. Just make sure to find out what the procedure is for transferring balances to the new cards.

Tip

Here are a couple of Web sites for finding good rates on credit cards, as well as rates on other things that might interest you. Remember, if you don't have a computer or aren't currently on the Internet, most libraries offer free Internet access — so you don't need to spend anything to view these sites.

- `www.getsmart.com`: Finds the lowest rates on credit cards and home loans.

- `www.bankrate.com`: Offers information on mortgages and the best credit card deals.

After you transfer balances from the higher-interest cards to the lower-interest cards, cut up the old cards, mail them back to the banks, stores, or companies that issued them, and close the accounts. The only potential exceptions are the cards necessary for identification, business, or emergencies (the cards with a zero balance), as discussed in Chapter 4. Otherwise, do "plastic surgery" and get rid of as many cards as possible.

Don't just throw them out. You need to mail the cut-up cards back to the banks to get the accounts closed and off your credit report.

Credit union loans

If you belong to a credit union, find out what types of loans are available. You may be able to get a personal loan at a rate far lower than what you're paying in credit card interest and use the money to pay off high-interest cards. (Don't forget to add repayment of the loan to your budget.) If you've been a member in good standing for some time, you could even get a loan at a rate lower than what a bank would offer. The credit union may even offer a bill-payer loan or consolidation loan — however, see Chapter 7 before considering this option.

Mortgage refinancing

If you have a mortgage that can be paid off early with no penalty, then refinancing is a possibility if interest rates drop. Refinancing your home consists of taking out another loan at a lower rate to pay off the earlier, higher-rate mortgage. (As with any mortgage procedure, you're charged fees, so take this into account when refinancing. Find out whether the costs can be rolled into the mortgage while still offering reduced monthly payments.)

Refinancing a mortgage is advantageous in that it not only can free up money for your current difficulties, but also can lower your payments for the duration of the mortgage, which helps you get your monthly debt obligation closer to that desirable 25 percent figure.

You can start by talking to your bank. For the best mortgage rates, however, you need to shop around. The financial section of your local newspaper should contain a listing of comparative mortgage rates in your area. The Web sites listed earlier in this chapter also give mortgage rate information. In addition, you can head online to check out the Mortgage Market at `www.interest.com/mmis.html`. This site offers online information about refinancing and government loans.

If refinancing your mortgage can free up enough money to help you, doing so is a much better deal than taking out a home equity loan (see the following section), because home equity loans carry interest rates that are a couple of points higher than the current mortgage interest rates.

Even if you think that you'll need a home equity loan, too, look into refinancing your mortgage before you consider a home equity loan. If interest rates are low, you may be surprised at how much you save, and you may decide against the loan. Plus, it's harder to refinance your mortgage once you have a second mortgage on the house.

Considering Home Equity Loans

If you've been in your home for a few years, you may have built up considerable equity. (Talk to the bank or lender that issued your mortgage to find out how much equity you currently have.) Using that equity can help get you out of debt, but some potential dangers are involved. Also, always remember that a home equity loan (formerly known as a second mortgage) is sort of like "unbuying" your house, and you have to buy it back again. Your equity is reduced by the amount you borrow.

Think about these pros and cons if you're considering a home equity loan:

- **Pro:** Like a mortgage, a home equity loan offers one of the few interest payments still recognized by the IRS as a deduction on your federal tax return. Also, if you negotiate a good rate, the interest rates can be considerably lower than those on many other forms of debt, especially credit cards.

- **Con:** If you haven't curtailed your bad spending practices and haven't stuck to a budget, you're putting your home in jeopardy. Unless you've already demonstrated both a willingness and an ability to spend only what is necessary, don't put your home at risk. If you think that not having much to spend is a drag, think of what a drag it would be to be *homeless* and not have much to spend.

If you decide that you're ready for a home equity loan and feel certain that you're not risking more than you want to lose, go ahead and get the loan. But get only as much as you need to cover your debts. Don't get anything extra.

Refuse to give in to the temptation to buy something else with money that you may see as being there for the spending. It's not. You have to pay it back. A home equity loan is a less expensive debt than a credit card, but it's not "found money." It's plain-old debt in a different disguise.

If, on the other hand, your total available equity doesn't cover all your debts — well, I think you know what to do by now. Pay off those credit cards, the highest ones first.

"Finding" More Money

You can look in a number of places for extra money — not all of them easy, but all worth considering.

The first thing to do is to review your nonessential expenses (listed in the budget that you created in Chapter 3). Scrutinize anything not related to your actual survival. You may want to review your essential expenses, too, to determine whether all of them are really essential (for example, do you have a lawn service because you hate mowing, or are you really unable to do the mowing yourself?).

In the sections that follow, you'll find lots of ideas about how to further chip away at your expenses. You may think that these small things won't make much of a difference, but consider this: If you have a 30-year mortgage of $100,000 at 8 percent, adding just $1 per day to your payment can save you $27,000 in interest and cut 4 years off the duration of the loan. These changes may look small, but they can have a huge impact in the long run.

So take small steps seriously and start looking for that extra money that has been getting away from you. When you get into the swing of things, you'll probably think of other areas in which you can cut back or other projects that you can do to save or earn money.

Reducing essential variable expenses

Learning to reduce essential variable expenses is one way that most people, even those who are not in debt, try to cut down on their monthly expenses. Getting good at this is useful even after you reach your goals. Here are some ideas:

- ■ Learn to prepare more frugal meals. Switching to cheap, nutritious foods like beans and rice can dramatically reduce your food budget. Also, drinking water instead of soft drinks can save you a fortune.

- ■ Start using coupons and shopping for bargains. (However, don't drive miles and miles to save 2 cents on milk, because you'll burn more in gas than you'll save.)

- Never go to the grocery store hungry, because you'll tend to buy more than you intended.

- Buy generic food, household goods, medications — anything available in generic form, if it saves you money.

- Change automobile insurance companies to receive a lower monthly premium.

- Wear a sweater instead of turning up the heat, or open the windows instead of running the air conditioner. A few degrees of difference in temperature can make a significant difference in your heating and cooling bills.

- Learn to do minor repairs and home maintenance jobs yourself.

- Repair or mend items rather than replacing them.

- Walk, carpool, or take public transportation when possible to save money on gasoline.

Changing your (expensive) habits

Your habits can have a huge impact on the outflow of money. Consider these examples:

- If you smoke, quit. A two-packs-a-day habit, at $2 a pack, translates into $1,400 per year.

- Stop drinking alcohol. As with smoking, what seems like a negligible amount of money adds up swiftly.

- Head to the public library rather than purchasing books at a bookstore. In addition to books, you can check out videos, cassette tapes, and CDs for free.

- Take your lunch to work. Dining even in an inexpensive restaurant can add a couple of dollars a day to your expenses. Bring your own coffee, too, unless your company supplies it for free.

■ Go to movies only during matinee hours or after they hit the discount theaters. You can also rent videos or — better yet — get them for free from the library.

Adding more cash to your cash flow

You can look for, or earn, more money in a variety of other places:

■ Increase your withholding allowance. If you normally get a refund from your income taxes, increase your withholding allowance. You may not get a refund next year, but your take-home pay will increase.

■ Look for a checking account that requires a lower minimum balance for free checking. If you switch from a bank that has a $1,500 minimum to one with a $1,000 minimum, you can apply the $500 to paying off debts.

■ Hold a garage sale. Or if you have items that are more valuable than the usual garage-sale stuff, try selling them through the newspaper, by posting a note on the bulletin board at work, or on the Internet.

■ Get a part-time job or tutor or consult in a field in which you excel.

■ If you're doing good work, ask for a raise.

■ Find out whether you can get vacation pay instead of taking time off. Even folks who are broke need time off, but doing this for part of your vacation time might help you along.

■ Rent out a spare room.

■ Barter. for example, find a friend or acquaintance who will baby-sit your kids in return for your mowing their lawn, or vice versa. The possibilities are almost limitless.

Cutting to the quick

If you've cut back everything else and you still can't make ends meet, you may have to do something about your essential expenses. Consider the following ideas:

■ If you have two cars, sell one. Take public transportation or carpool. If you must have two cars, see if you can downgrade — get a vehicle with lower payments.

■ If your financial situation is *really* bad, consider selling your house and buying either a smaller house or a condo. Remember, it's better to sell your home than to have it taken away, because then you have nothing. This suggestion applies only if you have cut *all* nonessential expenses and still can't make your monthly payments.

■ If you're paying alimony or child support to a former spouse who is doing better than you are financially, you may be able to apply for a reduction in those payments.

Some of these measures may seem drastic, but they're not nearly as drastic, or as potentially damaging, as bankruptcy (which you can learn more about in Chapter 7). The measures in this chapter might inconvenience you, but they won't destroy your credit history or ruin your life.

CHAPTER 6

GETTING HELP

- Getting counseling for your money and other problems
- Looking at programs that have helped others
- Discovering what help the government may offer
- Avoiding situations that can sabotage your success

Sometimes, things get to be more than you can handle alone. Depending on how deeply you're in debt and/or how you got into debt, you can turn to numerous programs, organizations, and individuals that can give you a hand — either financially or emotionally.

Refer to your worksheet from Chapter 2 on how you got into debt, as well as your list of outstanding debts, to determine which of the sources in this chapter might be appropriate for you. Be honest with yourself as you review this information, and seek the help that's appropriate for your situation.

Debt Counseling and Other Debt Help

Debt counselors can be useful if you find that you simply can't make the figures in your budget work. Also, for some people, having someone give them assignments or hold them accountable works better than doing it on their own.

Although a lot of debt counselors also offer consolidations, some services that identify themselves as debt counselors are really just consolidators. All counselors need information about your budget and amount of debt in order to help you, but make sure that you know what you're getting into before you supply detailed information, such as the names of your creditors or credit card account numbers. (See the section on consolidations in Chapter 7 before you make any decisions regarding consolidating, even if your counselor recommends that approach.)

Here are some places to look for debt counselors:

■ Take advantage of an Employee Assistance Program (EAP). Check with your employer's human resources department to see whether your company offers such a program. These plans offer company-paid counseling for a wide range of difficulties, from job burnout to alcoholism to debt. Participation is confidential, so you don't have to worry about information getting back to your employer.

■ One of the many organizations that falls into that category of both counselor and consolidator is the Consumer Credit Counseling Service (CCCS). You can find a listing for a local office of this nationwide, not-for-profit organization in the white pages of your phone book or on the Internet — but *do not* contact them until you've read the section on consolidators in Chapter 7.

■ Talk to your banker. Your bank may offer a debt-counseling program or may be able to recommend one.

■ Talk to your accountant, tax specialist, lawyer, or financial planner, if you have one. Solicit his or her input, or get recommendations for debt counselors.

■ Check the Internet for debt counselors and other sources related to debt.

Many debt counselors and financial planners have written books or recorded videos or audio tapes about debt recovery. Libraries and bookstores are full of titles that may help you get through both the financial and emotional aspects of debt recovery. See the CliffsNotes Resource Center at the back of this book for a couple of titles to consider, though you may find others you like (ask for recommendations, because new books come out all the time).

A considerable amount of software has been designed to help you with the numbers when you're working on debts or budgets. If your only worry is getting the numbers right, these products may be all you need. Of course, if you're really broke, you're probably better off using the free calculators that you may be able to find online, but if you have some discretionary income left in your budget, financial software may be something you want to consider.

Personal Counseling

Sometimes, uncontrolled spending reveals deep-seated wounds or emotional needs. You may be escaping loneliness, depression, or fear or avoiding the need to face behavior that's hurting you. Perhaps you haven't learned appropriate ways of dealing with stress. You may feel exhilarated when you've been out on a spending spree. Or pursuing the newest or biggest or best may help you anesthetize feelings of inadequacy. There are myriad reasons people get out of control, but no matter what reasons lie behind your spending, you can find a solution to your problem.

Counseling can be a good way to deal with the problems behind the spending, but what if you can't cover the expense? You still have options:

■ Check with your company's human resources department to see whether your employer offers an Employee Assistance Program (EAP).

■ Find out whether your health insurance covers counseling. Most comprehensive policies include some counseling or emotional- or psychological-recovery services.

■ If you attend a church or synagogue, find out whether counseling is available there. Often, it is free or offered on a sliding scale based on what you can afford.

■ If you have a bit of discretionary income available (or if some becomes available as you progress toward getting out of debt), you may want to spend some of it on counseling. There are counseling agencies that offer discounts for people who can't pay the full (and often considerable) cost for a counselor.

■ Join a support group or discussion group. (See the section that follows for suggestions.)

■ Talk to friends who have been through situations or traumas similar to your own. Often, just talking through a problem contributes to the solution.

Maybe you don't need the help of a professional — at least not in the flesh. A wide range of books, videos, and audio tapes are available on working your way through a wide range of problems, from a simple lack of discipline to recovery from abuse or emotional disorders. Don't worry that this is a "second rate" choice — studies have shown that an individual who is determined to change can be just as successful using alternative methods as those who seek professional help. Alternative methods can include anything from talking to friends to soul-searching to reading a good self-help book.

So whichever method, or combination of methods, works best for you — from private counseling to a good book on helping yourself recover — do seek the healing that will help make everything, including debt recovery, easier, happier, and healthier.

12-Step and Other Recovery Programs

If you need help recovering from anything that you do to excess, whether it's spending too much money or indulging in some activity to a degree that affects your income, you can probably find a group to help you.

A wide range of 12-step programs is available, for everything from simple debt recovery to help for a wide range of emotional disorders. Because debt can be triggered by something deeper than just not understanding compound interest, you may find that you need recovery from something that is more than merely financial. Alcoholics Anonymous is the best known of the 12-step programs, but it's not alone anymore. As the success of 12-step programs has spread, the programs have multiplied, all employing the basic steps of the original program. Now, other recovery groups are popping up. The benefit of these programs is that they offer both guidelines for recovery and the emotional support of a network of friends and acquaintances in a similar situation.

These programs also offer you a framework that may be invaluable to your recovery. If your spending — or any other aspect of your life — is out of control and you need more than just helpful hints, the sense of accountability, fellowship, and more structured environment that a recovery program offers may be the key that helps you get on track and stay there.

You can find local chapters of the most popular and successful programs by checking the white pages of your local phone directory. You can also use the Internet to help you find more information about the groups, or to find meetings wherever you may travel. Here is an alphabetical listing of some of the more common 12-step programs, along with their Web addresses, plus Web addresses for links to myriad other programs across the nation and around the world:

- **Alcoholics Anonymous:** `www.alcoholics-anonymous.org`.

- **AL-ANON:** `www.al-anon.org` (for family members of alcoholics).

- **AnonymousOne:** `www.sobertoo.com/main.htm` (not officially associated with the 12-step programs). This recovery resource offers links to thousands of meetings, treatment centers, 12-step programs, activities and events, success stories, and a newsletter.

- **Debtors Anonymous:** `debtorsanonymous.org`.

- **Emotions Anonymous:** `www.emotionsanonymous.org`.

- **Gamblers Anonymous:** `www.gamblersanonymous.org`.

- **Recovery Network:** `www.recoverynetwork.com/links/index.html`. This site offers chat rooms, recovery and prevention links, 12-step programs, government resources, support groups, and more.

- **Recovery Online:** `www.recovery.alano.org`. This site offers links to just about every self-help recovery group online, even identifying programs by religious (or nonreligious) preferences.

- **12stepmeetings.com:** `www.12stepmeetings.com`. This site can help you find a meeting, no matter where you're going, and even offers the option of meeting online if you just can't get out.

Don't underestimate the importance of going to meetings. A sense of community and accountability is an important part of recovery.

If circumstances make going to regular meetings impractical for you, you can pick up one of the many books based on the 12 steps, including the original classic created for Alcoholics

Anonymous. So if you can't get to a meeting or you don't have Internet access, you can still benefit from the wisdom and experience of these groups.

Government Assistance

The government offers a wide range of assistance, both during and after your debt crisis. You can find everything from information to financial aid among the many government departments and services designed to help consumers.

U.S. Department of Housing and Urban Development

Better known as *HUD,* the U.S. Department of Housing and Urban Development can offer you considerable help while you're in financial straits. Whether you own a home that you're afraid of losing, you want to refinance, you can't afford rent in your area, or you just can't come up with enough of a down payment to get started in home ownership, this department has agencies and programs that can help.

You can find the phone number and address of your local HUD office by looking in the Government-Federal section of the phone book. However, the easiest way to explore what HUD has to offer is on the Internet. Access its site at www.hud.gov and click on the subject that interests you. You may want to start by clicking on Own a Home or Rental Help.

Under Own a Home, you'll find links to Keeping Your Home (which includes avoiding foreclosure) and Refinancing. Both links give more information about the Housing Counseling Agencies. These agencies are designed to help you find the financing or assistance you need so that you don't lose your home.

For information about what the Housing Counseling Agencies can do for you, call 800-217-6970.

The Rental Help option offers information about Federal Rental Assistance and Low Income Housing that may be available to you. Because the definition of low income is based on the median income for your area, you may be surprised by what constitutes low income where you live. Even if you don't want to rely on government aid long-term or don't particularly want to live in the type of minimal housing that the program offers, this assistance might help you get back on your feet if your financial situation is severe.

Internal Revenue Service

Despite what some people think, the IRS really doesn't want to ruin your life. Of course, your best bet is always to pay all your taxes on time. However, if circumstances have become overwhelming and you're in trouble with the IRS, help is available. One section of the IRS, the Taxpayer Advocate, has the power to intervene in any case where significant hardship would result from action taken by the IRS.

(A legal action put into motion by the IRS can end in a number of situations that could cause hardship, such as the suspension of your business, garnishment of your wages, or the need to hire costly representation to defend you against the IRS in court.)

If an IRS action would prevent you from being able to afford basic necessities, like housing, food, transportation, and utilities, you can get help. Form 911 is the Application for Taxpayer Assistance; it's the way you enlist the aid of the Taxpayer Advocate.

This option really applies only in extreme circumstances and is not a way to get out of paying taxes just because you're behind on your bills. However, applying for Taxpayer

Assistance can keep you from having the IRS take any action that would interfere with your survival. The IRS will want to "help" you put together a budget and repayment plan (and will in all likelihood have a stricter definition of nonessential expenses than you do), because they do still want their money. But you'll have a place to live, something to eat, and a way to get to work.

To find out more about the Taxpayer Advocate, Form 911, or Taxpayer Assistance, you can access the IRS Web site at `www.irs.ustreas.gov/prod/ind_info/advocate.html`. You can also call the IRS during regular business hours at 800-829-1040 for general information or 800-829-3676 to request forms (such as Form 911), documents, and tax-related publications.

Freddie Mac and Fannie Mae

The nicknames Freddie Mac and Fannie Mae represent two different but related government corporations. *Freddie Mac* is the Federal Home Loan Mortgage Corporation, and *Fannie Mae* is the Federal National Mortgage Association.

Although these entities don't offer the kind of "get out of trouble" assistance that HUD offers, they're good sources of loans once you're on the other side of your debt problems. Freddie Mac and Fannie Mae specialize in making mortgages available to those who have less than the standard 20 percent down payment, and they can help you start building an improved credit history.

Most real estate agents know about loans available from these organizations and from HUD, so when you get to the point where you start considering buying a house, you can talk to them about the help available here. For more information, you can access these government entities online at `www.freddiemac.com` and `www.fanniemae.com`.

Veterans Administration and the Department of Veterans Affairs

If you're a veteran of the U.S. military, the Veterans Administration (VA) offers a wide range of services that may be useful to you. The VA and Department of Veterans Affairs operate hospitals and offer home loans, disability compensation, and pensions to veterans.

You can find local offices for both of these government departments in your phone directory under Government.

Consumer Information Center

This government department offers assistance in the form of abundant, valuable information. View the majority of the center's reports for free at its Web site, www.pueblo. gsa.gov. Print versions of all reports are also available for a nominal fee (or for free, in the case of the Consumer Resource Handbook); order online or write to Consumer Information Center, Dept. WWW, Pueblo, CO 81009, or call 888-8PUEBLO (888-878-3256).

The first thing you should get your hands on is the current Consumer Resource Handbook. You can order this book from the center or download it from the center's Web site (about 150 pages, so it takes a bit of time). Or you can just keep referring to the handbook at the Web site.

This handbook includes information about consumer-related federal, state, and local government offices; Better Business Bureaus; ways to avoid consumer and investment fraud; and just about anything else you need to be an informed consumer.

If you access the center's Web site, click on Housing to access reports on topics like saving energy, refinancing your mortgage, and home maintenance. Or click on Money for information about getting the best buys, making sense of savings, and avoiding telemarketing swindles. The And More button leads to information about avoiding online scams.

U.S. Consumer Gateway

The U.S. Consumer Gateway is another source of a wealth of information. However, this resource is available only via the Internet, at www.consumer.gov. This site can connect you to any federal agency that deals with consumer issues.

The Your Home page offers tips on saving money on utilities and reducing energy consumption, plus links to government departments offering mortgages. The Your Money page has a good section on credit and investor education and a scam alert.

Beware of Scams

Warning

When you're looking for help, you're often a target. Scam artists know that you're worried, and they hope you're so scared that you've stopped thinking. However, a few guidelines can help you avoid a lot of problems — not just the scammers who prey on folks in debt.

The two overarching principles to keep in mind are these: First, if it seems too good to be true, it is. Second, don't do business with an organization that you've never heard of until you've taken the time to check it out. Here are some tips on how this works out in real life, along with some examples of scams you may encounter:

- If a business making an offer to you gives you a company name, check it out with the Better Business Bureau.

■ Beware of anything that directs you to make a phone call to a 900 number in order to "complete the transaction." (Local 976 and long-distance 700 numbers can be as costly as 900 numbers.) Don't call.

■ Phone fraud is common. Ask to see the offer in writing, especially if you don't know the organization well. If they refuse, say, "Thank you, but I'm not interested," and hang up *quickly,* before they have a chance to continue the high-pressure sales pitch.

■ If a consolidator offers to make all your problems go away, make *the consolidator* go away. It's *never* that easy. (Read Chapter 7 on how to find consolidators who aren't scammers.)

■ Question the validity of any organization that offers huge benefits, such as free vacations, "just for looking." This is a common way for companies to lure consumers into expense transactions. The prize catches your interest and gets you into their offices; then they use high-pressure techniques to try to get you to buy land, time-shares, or travel packages. Often, if you don't buy (the packages they're selling can cost tens of thousands of dollars), you won't get the prize. Or you'll get the plane tickets, but you'll have to stay at their expensive resort to use them. Even if you get out without spending anything, you'll have endured hours of high-pressure sales. No prize is worth that.

■ Know your rights. For example, according to the Fair Credit and Charge Card Disclosure Act, a credit card company is required to tell you the interest rate, annual fee, grace period, any additional charges, and method for calculating the balance on which finance charges are based. If you get an offer that doesn't include this information, it's bogus. Toss it.

■ Find out where you can check on scams and swindles. Here are a few possibilities:

The Consumer Information Center (`www.pueblo. gsa.gov`) particularly focuses on telemarketing swindles.

The Credit Information Center (`www.creditinfo-center.com`) has a Scam Update page to help you identify consolidation scams.

The U.S. Consumer Gateway (`www.consumer.gov`) offers scam alerts under its "Your Money" heading.

Warning

If someone pressures you by saying that you'll miss an opportunity or that it won't be available tomorrow, flee immediately. Real services are there for the long term and *want* you to check them out.

CHAPTER 7
TAKING DRASTIC MEASURES

IN THIS CHAPTER

- Knowing how the law protects you
- Working with your creditors
- Examining the pros and cons of consolidating

If debt has taken you well beyond the point of being merely uncomfortable and into the realm of serious concern — and possibly even trouble — you need to know your rights and options. You can do a lot to give yourself breathing room while you work to get your finances under control.

Knowing Your Rights

A number of laws protect you as a consumer of credit and as a debtor. Some laws protect you against discrimination when applying for a loan, and others guarantee that credit card companies will supply you with information regarding interest rates and grace periods. The laws presented in this section are the ones most likely to be useful for someone in debt.

Fair Debt Collection Practices Act

The Fair Debt Collection Practices Act protects you from potentially abusive practices by collection agencies. This act applies only to agencies or individuals that collect debts for others, and not to businesses or individuals trying to collect their own accounts.

This law was designed to protect individuals and covers personal, family, and household debts, including money owed for charge accounts, medical expenses, and the purchase of a car.

Generally, a business turns an account over for collection when it is three months past due (unless you have contacted the company to make arrangements for payment). This act protects you after the account goes to a collection agency.

Following are the primary stipulations of the act:

- A debt collector may contact you by mail, telephone, telegram, or in person, but not at inconvenient or unusual times or places, unless you agree.

- A debt collector can't contact you at work if the agency has been informed that your employer disapproves of such contact.

- The initial letter must state the amount of debt and the name of the original creditor. The letter must also state that you have 30 days to dispute the validity of the debt.

If the amount is incorrect and you wish to dispute it, do so immediately — in writing. Include your name and account number and any information about the account that pertains to the dispute. If documentation exists that supports your claim, include a photocopy (never the original) with your letter.

- If you send a letter disputing a debt, the collection agency may not contact you again until the dispute is settled.

- If the debt is not an error, the agency sends you verification from the original creditor (such as a copy of the bill). At this time, collection activities begin again.

- A collection agency is limited in whom it can contact: If you have an attorney, a debt collector can contact only you or the attorney. If you have no attorney, the collector may contact other people, but only to find out where you live or work. Usually, the collector is not allowed to tell anyone other than you or your attorney that you owe money.

■ Debt collectors may not harass you, which means that they may not use threats of violence, threaten to ruin your reputation, advertise or publish your debt, use obscene or profane language, or phone repeatedly just to annoy you.

■ Debt collectors may not make false statements in order to collect a debt. They are not allowed to . . .

. . . Use a false name when contacting you or others or falsely imply that they are attorneys or government agents

. . . Falsely imply that you have committed a crime or state that papers being sent are legal forms if they are not

. . . Misrepresent the amount of your debt or give false credit information about you to anyone

. . . Say that the nonpayment of debt will result in arrest, *garnishment* (a legal procedure whereby part of your wages are withheld to satisfy a creditor), *attachment* (seizure by legal process of property or funds), or similar unless they intend to take legal action (if they intend to take legal action, however, these are possible outcomes)

. . . Threaten to take any action that cannot legally be taken

■ Unfair practices are also prohibited, which means that collection agencies may not

. . . Collect more money than you owe

. . . Make you accept collect calls

. . . Deposit a postdated check before the date on the check

. . . Contact you by postcard

. . . Add on finance charges or service fees in collecting a debt unless you authorized the extra charge in the agreement that created the debt

■ If a debt collector represents several of your creditors, you may specify to which accounts payments should be applied.

■ If you don't want to hear further from a collection agency about a debt that you cannot currently pay, you can write a letter stating that you want the agency to stop contacting you. (Be sure to keep a copy for your files.) As soon as the agency receives such a letter, it must stop all communication except to notify you that it received the letter and to notify you when any action will be taken.

Your letter should be businesslike. Address the letter to the individual who is your primary contact at the agency. Include the date, your full name, and your account number before the salutation. The body of the letter should acknowledge that they have contacted you and explain that you are unable to pay the bill(s) at this time. Then note that you are aware of your rights under the Fair Debt Collection Practices Act and ask that, as provided by the act, you are giving them formal notice that you wish to have them discontinue communications. Close with "Sincerely," and sign your name.

If you believe that a debt collector has violated any of these provisions, contact the firm's management, especially if you feel that the agency is normally reliable and that a specific collector's behavior is unrepresentative. However, if you don't get swift and satisfactory action from management, or if the violation is serious, report the problem to your state's attorney general's office. Often, additional debt collection laws exist at the state level, and the attorney general's office can help you determine your rights as well as make sure that they are protected.

Fair Credit Reporting Act

The Fair Credit Reporting Act, which was designed to protect consumers against the circulation of inaccurate or obsolete information, gives consumers legal access to their credit reports. This act is particularly important if you've been denied credit, insurance, or employment based on your credit report, because it requires lenders and others to give you contact information for any credit bureau or consumer reporting agency that they consulted. You can then find out whether your credit report is accurate and up-to-date.

This act also makes it possible for people who are trying to improve their credit histories to find out precisely what their credit reports contain. Although you may not be interested in seeing one of these reports while your credit is in its worst shape, you may wish to request one as you get closer to your goal. You may also want to request another one a year after you reach your goal to see how the report has improved and to make sure that no obsolete information remains.

A credit report can

■ Help you discover whether you have any credit cards that you're not using but that still show up as active (Cancel those cards — too much available credit makes lenders nervous.)

■ Reveal any unresolved errors

■ Help you confirm that accounts have been closed or that positive information has been recorded

If you find an error or obsolete information, you're protected by the Consumer Credit Reporting Reform Act, which the next section covers.

If and when you decide that you want a copy of your credit report, you can contact any credit bureau, and for a fee of $8 to $12, they will supply one. You can find the names of local agencies in the Yellow Pages under "Credit" or "Credit Rating or Reporting Agencies."

Here are the phone numbers for the three largest and most commonly used credit bureaus in the United States:

- Trans Union, 800-916-8800

- Experian (formerly TRW), 800-682-7654

- CBI-Equifax, 800-685-1111

Credit reports have been designed to provide information in a way that creditors, who need the information for decision-making, can easily read and understand. The report identifies you by name, address, date of birth, and social security number. Your employer is also listed.

A summary of your outstanding debts is included, and if any amount is past due, the amount is noted. Various elements, like open credit card accounts, public record items, and collection items, are grouped together by type. You also find a list of past requests made for the report, so you can see who has checked your credit record.

If you have any difficulty reading the report or have questions about how entries should be interpreted, call the customer service department of the bureau from which you requested the report.

Consumer Credit Reporting Reform Act

If you do find an error on your credit report, the Consumer Credit Reporting Reform Act makes it easier for you to correct it. If you bring an error to the attention of a credit bureau, they must investigate it within 30 days. If they cannot disprove your claim, they must remove the information from your report.

If you believe that your credit report contains obsolete information, particularly if you feel that the erroneous information has resulted in your being denied credit, insurance, or employment, here are the steps to take:

1. Ask the lender, insurance agent, or employer to give you the contact information for the credit bureau they consulted.

2. Contact the credit bureau and get a copy of your report.

3. Study the report for inaccuracies or obsolete information.

4. Report any errors you find *in writing* to the credit bureau. Notify the credit bureau of any errors, whether you requested the report because you were denied credit or just to confirm the status of your credit history.

5. If you find no errors but feel that your credit problems were caused by unusual circumstances, send an explanation. The law allows you to have a 100-word statement attached to your credit report, so write an explanation of any exceptional circumstances surrounding late or unpaid accounts and send it to the credit bureau.

Dealing with Creditors

Both before and after people start calling and asking you for money, you can take action to improve your situation. The key to dealing with creditors is to be honest and open with them. You don't have to reveal every detail of your life, but you must clearly relate the facts that affect your ability to repay your debt.

First and most important, if you suddenly find yourself in a position where you can't pay bills (for example, if you lose your job or have overwhelming medical bills), immediately contact all creditors (utility companies, credit card companies, and so on). Let them know that you're experiencing financial difficulties. More than likely, your creditors will allow you to miss one or two payments if they know that you'll be able to repay in the near future, or they may permit reduced payments during the crisis.

If you already have bills past due and you haven't contacted your creditors, do so as soon as possible. Understand that silence on your part is viewed as reluctance to pay bills. However, taking the initiative and contacting creditors first is viewed as an indication that you take your debts seriously and are committed to making efforts to repay. By talking to your creditors, you may be able to make arrangements that keep accounts from being turned over to collection agencies.

Remember

Remember that the jobs of the people with whom you speak depend on collecting debts, so you may need to be firm and persistent. However, they do want to retain you as a customer, and they understand that slow repayment is better than no repayment.

Unsecured debts offer you the greatest opportunity for negotiating because

■ No collateral is involved in unsecured debts (such as credit cards), so these creditors don't have an easy solution to their problems. Because they have no property to repossess, they must recover money to stay in business.

■ Credit card companies know that they can earn more interest from you if you take longer to repay your debt, so they're often willing to reduce the amount of your minimum payment.

■ Businesses that want to keep you as a client may be willing to lower your interest rates or reduce your payments.

Contacting creditors as soon as possible is vital. With credit cards, for example, you start receiving notices and collection calls as soon as you miss a payment date, and an entry is made at that time on your credit report. Credit card issuers can cancel your card when your account reaches 45 to 60 days overdue, depending on the company's policy. And all creditors will be happier with you if they feel that you're making a conscious effort to get them some money.

Talking to your credit card company

If, after you work out your budget and cut every possible nonessential expense, you find that you don't have enough money to cover your minimum payments, asking your credit card companies for a reduction in minimum payments would be worthwhile. To do so, you need to do a bit of work:

1. Make a list of all your credit cards.

2. Next to the name of each card, write the account number, balance due, and minimum payment.

3. Total the minimum payments due for all cards.

4. Determine by how much you must reduce this total in order for the payments to fit into your budget.

5. Next to each minimum payment, write a proposed minimum that enables you to reduce the total slightly more than necessary (to give yourself room to negotiate, in case the companies do not accept your proposed amounts). Be reasonable, however — you can reduce $75 to $50, but not to $1.

6. Telephone the credit card company. (The toll-free number should be on the credit card or bill.) Ask for customer service, and then ask to speak to a supervisor — supervisors have the authority to handle such situations.

7. Explain the situation and propose the amount you have calculated as your minimum payment. Be firm. If necessary, remind the supervisor that you're in financial difficulty and that if you're forced into bankruptcy, the company will get no money.

Also, be willing to negotiate — if you suggest $50 instead of $75 and they say $55, you're still ahead $20. If they say $60, you can suggest $55.

Be polite and friendly. Customer service agents are not required to accommodate you, but they're more likely to want to help if you're pleasant.

8. Keep your list in front of you so that you can note the amount you settle on during the negotiation. Also record the date and the name of the person with whom you have been speaking.

9. Immediately send a letter to the person you spoke with (keeping a copy for your files) outlining your agreement, along with a promise that you'll increase the payment amount as soon as possible. Put your account number on the letter, and be sure to thank the individual for his or her understanding (no matter how difficult the negotiation was).

10. Make the payments you negotiated, and make them on time.

If at any time you have extra money, make a bigger payment on a credit card. Remember how quickly the interest builds up, how much less you'll pay, and how much you can reduce the repayment time by plowing extra cash (such as bonuses or unexpected income) into paying off credit cards.

Dealing with fixed loans

If negotiating lower minimum payments for credit cards doesn't get you to where you're working inside your budget, you may need to work with your fixed-loan payments (installment plans, personal loans, student loans, and the like).

As with the preceding credit card exercise, you need to create a worksheet that lists all outstanding fixed loans, including the name of the lender, the amount due, and the monthly payment. Contact the bank or loan company to whom you owe the debt and ask to talk to a loan officer or credit manager.

Explain your present difficulties and outline what you hope to accomplish, noting whether the situation is short-term or long-term. If it's likely that you'll be out of trouble in a short time, you can ask to have the monthly payments reduced for a few months.

Alternatively, you can ask if the lender will extend your loan for a longer period but with lower payments. This approach increases the amount of interest you pay, but if it makes it possible for you to continue to make payments and live within your budget, it's worth it. You'll protect your credit history while still living within your means.

In all other respects, this process is similar to that of negotiating with credit card companies. The job of loan officers and credit managers is to get loans paid, and as long as you're reasonable and show a real desire to pay off the debts, they'll generally want to work with you to reach a mutually satisfying agreement.

As always, the key is to faithfully pay the reduced amount that you negotiate.

Stopping repossession of your car

Now you're moving into the area of secured loans. This is a little trickier because something exists that a creditor can take away from you. If you start missing car payments, the creditor can and will repossess the car.

One of the biggest problems is that, if your car is repossessed (or even if you give it back), you still have to pay the *deficiency balance* when the car is sold. The deficiency balance is the difference between what you still owe on the loan and what the creditor can get for the car. So you could be without a car *and* still have an outstanding debt.

Two major reasons explain why creditors will more than likely be willing to work with you when it comes to a car loan. First, most people realize that a car is a necessity, and the creditor realizes that if you can't get to work, you won't ever repay the loan. Second, a car loses its value pretty quickly, and creditors know that it probably won't sell for much. And if you can't pay the loan, creditors know that you probably won't be able to pay the deficiency balance, but they charge it anyway. By doing so, they can get something from the settlement of your property if you declare bankruptcy.

Again, the key to avoiding this problem is to talk to the creditor. In this case, you may be talking to a bank or an auto loan company. Talk to a supervisor or loan officer. Explain your financial problems and ask for an extension. Generally, the loan company will allow you to go one, two, or even three months without making a payment, although they'll charge you additional interest on those payments and add both the payments and the extra interest to the end of your current contract.

Every auto loan company has a different set of rules for extensions. These rules might include a maximum of three months on extensions or a requirement that you have already made a specific number of payments. However, in a month or two with no car payments, you may be able to get ahead on other, higher-interest bills. You should also start setting aside what you can afford so that when the extension is up, you can start making payments again.

Considering Consolidators

Warning

When thinking about debt recovery, the first thing most people think of is *consolidating* — hiring a company or getting a loan that consolidates all their bills into one lump with smaller payments than they're making now. And there certainly are plenty of consolidators out there. But proceed with caution. There are good reasons to avoid consolidations — and useful strategies for deciding if and when you may want to use one.

The real problem may not get fixed

Unless you've corrected the behaviors that got you into debt, going the consolidation route will do far more harm than good.

■ Don't consider consolidation until you have lived successfully on a budget for six months or more. (See Chapter 3 for information about creating and maintaining a budget.) If you haven't changed your habits, consolidation won't help at all — and could make things worse.

■ Borrow only what you need to cover your outstanding debts. Don't give in to the temptation to get a little more for that special something that will end up plunging you deeper into the hole.

■ Don't think that consolidation gets you out of taking debt seriously. Some people actually spend more money the month after they get a consolidation loan because they think that their problems are solved.

Consolidators may not help as much as you hope

A common misconception is that consolidations resolve all your debt problems. This may not be the case.

- Consolidations are available only for unsecured debt, so if the majority of your debt is secured, a consolidation may not be an option.

- If you're using a consolidating service, you often have to pay a fee. You need to decide whether this money would help you more if you applied it to outstanding debts.

- The use of a consolidator is recorded on your credit record and may influence the decisions of future creditors who see it. If your debt is serious, having this information on your record may not be your biggest worry. However, if your debt is only a few thousand dollars, which you can pay off in a year or two with careful budgeting, you probably don't want to use a consolidator.

- Your monthly payments may be less, but repayment takes longer, so the interest may be far more than if you had just stuck with paying your bills.

Much of what consolidators do is negotiate lower payments with your creditors. Because you can handle this negotiation yourself (as described earlier in this chapter), why not avoid the consolidator's fee and the damaging note in your credit history?

If you do decide that you need to consolidate your debts, look at a variety of sources for consolidation funds, such as cash-value insurance, pledged collateral, credit unions, and family loans. When all is said and done, consolidation is still better than bankruptcy.

Tip

As a last resort, if no other source of funds is available and your debt is completely unmanageable without additional funds, consider withdrawing money from a retirement account. Be aware that you must pay a penalty of 10 percent and pay back taxes, so compare these costs to the costs of available consolidation loans. But even though you're putting your future somewhat in jeopardy, it's already in jeopardy if your debt is that bad. Depending on where you are in life (especially if you're relatively young), rebuilding the retirement fund may be easier than working with a ruined credit rating.

Not all consolidators are good consolidators

Many consolidators are honest and will help you with your debt situation (although the problems outlined in the preceding section may still apply). Unfortunately, however, because so many opportunities exist to make money at the expense of desperate debtors, some consolidators are less than honorable.

Some firms charge high fees and then do little or nothing to help you with your debts. Others neglect to use the money you send them to pay your bills, replying to your call that you're covering their expenses with your first payments (during which time your accounts get further past due).

To avoid running into these kinds of problems, search for reliable consolidators. Ask friends, associates, and debt counselors for recommendations; do an Internet search to learn about your options; or check a firm's background with the Better Business Bureau, *Consumer Reports,* or the Credit Information Center (www.creditinfocenter.com — look to the Scam Update page).

Be wary when shopping for consolidators. Avoid any consolidator who promises easy answers. Make sure to check the company's track record and get a report of *all* costs (fees and interest) before signing anything.

CHAPTER 8

LAST HOPE: FILING BANKRUPTCY

IN THIS CHAPTER

- Looking closely at why bankruptcy may not be a good choice

- Learning which debts are covered by bankruptcy and which aren't

- Reviewing the types of bankruptcy that apply to individuals

- Deciding whether bankruptcy is appropriate for you

When you say "debt," most people immediately think "bankruptcy." There is certainly an epidemic of personal bankruptcy in the United States today. But bankruptcy is not an easy solution. It can seriously disrupt your life, it ruins your credit history, and it's possible that it won't get rid of most of your debts. Make sure that you know all the facts before you consider this option.

Your Best Bet: Avoid Bankruptcy

Warning

If a chronic gambler deserts his wife and leaves her with a hefty mortgage, $90,000 in credit card debt, and six children, she might want to consider bankruptcy. For everyone else, bankruptcy is probably a bad choice. Here's why:

- Bankruptcy is humiliating. It seriously undercuts your sense of self-esteem and makes it difficult for you to make positive changes in your life.

■ You can lose much of your personal property. (The court sells the property to pay your creditors. If you're going to lose everything anyway, why not sell it yourself? You'll probably get a better price for it, and you won't have a bankruptcy ruining your credit report.)

■ The blot remains on your credit record for ten years, so you probably won't be able to take out loans, get credit cards, or do anything else that requires a review of your credit record.

■ If a friend or relative cosigned a loan, he or she is not protected by your bankruptcy and will have to repay your debts.

■ Bankruptcy takes away the safety net of security that credit can supply your family.

■ Bankruptcy hurts innocent people who trusted you to repay. It has a major impact on merchants and lenders and can, in the long run, mean job loss or business closure.

■ You aren't likely to learn the necessary lessons to keep you from repeating your folly. In fact, 50 percent of the people who file bankruptcy file it again later in their lives, because they have changed no patterns and learned no new skills.

■ Filing for bankruptcy costs money (attorney and court fees), and that money may be better spent elsewhere.

■ You expose your financial lifestyle to the public. Your bankruptcy petition, schedules, and payment plan are public documents, available to the general public at the bankruptcy clerk's office, and the foreclosure on your mortgage is published in the Public Notices section of the local paper.

■ Any job that involves being bonded (bank teller, jewelry clerk, and so on) may be in jeopardy.

Many of these points apply only if your filing is successful, which is not necessarily guaranteed. If you fail to follow any of the necessary steps, such as showing up for the creditors' meeting, answering the court's questions honestly and completely, or producing the necessary books and records, the case can be dismissed. If this happens, you still owe everything you did before you started, but you're out the attorney and court fees.

Today, too many people are filing for bankruptcy to escape debt that is merely inconvenient. The courts are getting stricter and are looking more closely at all cases. Judges are on the lookout for people who are simply trying to get out of paying their bills, as opposed to those who are truly suffering hardship. If a judge determines that you have enough income to cover the monthly payments for your debts, and especially if you have any discretionary income left after making those payments, it's likely that your bankruptcy case will be thrown out of court.

Who Benefits from Bankruptcy?

The person most likely to benefit from bankruptcy is the attorney who talks you into it or whom you hire to file for you. Attorney's fees can be substantial. If you try the do-it-yourself kits and guidebooks, whoever created or is selling the kit benefits. Bankruptcy benefits the debtor only occasionally, and never benefits society as a whole.

Sometimes, however, situations arise that are so devastating that bankruptcy appears to be the only survivable choice. If your mortgage is being foreclosed and your car is being repossessed, filing for Chapter 13 bankruptcy may give you breathing space while allowing you to hang onto your property. (Details on the different types of bankruptcy appear later in this chapter.)

If you have no possible way to repay your debts in your lifetime, and all your debts (or at least the majority of them) fall into the category of dischargeable debt, and if you really have no other options and no available funds, then you may need to consider Chapter 7 bankruptcy. But bankruptcy is not an easy way out.

Understanding Which Debts Are Dischargeable and Which Are Nondischargeable

Not all debts go away when you file for bankruptcy. Most unsecured debts are *dischargeable,* which means that you are no longer legally required to repay them. However, some unsecured debts are *nondischargeable* — that is, you still have to repay them even after filing for bankruptcy. For secured debts, you surrender the property that you used as collateral, or pay the debt if you want to retain the collateral.

Which type of debt you have determines whether you have anything to gain from declaring bankruptcy.

- **Dischargeable debts** include, but are not limited to, credit card purchases, rent, and medical bills.

- **Nondischargeable debts** include, but are not limited to, student loans, alimony or child support, taxes, properly executed contracts involving titles or liens, debts incurred as a result of drunk driving, and eve-of-bankruptcy spending sprees (or any substantial purchases close to the time of filing).

In addition, after you file for bankruptcy, your creditors have 60 days to object. If they file a suit, it's possible that a discharge will be denied for the debt in question.

However, you can't really guess what the judge will decide about your creditors' suits (unless you know that one of your creditors is in worse shape financially than you are), but you should be able to identify your dischargeable debts. If that's what most of your debts are, then bankruptcy can help reduce your debt burden — but don't forget that it doesn't make your problems go away.

Looking at the Types of Bankruptcy

Several different types of bankruptcy exist, each identified by the number of the chapter of the Bankruptcy Code in which it is defined. However, only two types are likely to apply to you as an individual debtor (as opposed to a business or farm): Chapter 7 and Chapter 13.

If you do come to the point of bankruptcy, find out whether you can file Chapter 13. Avoid Chapter 7 if possible, because it's the more damaging.

Chapter 7

Chapter 7 bankruptcy is personal financial dissolution, also known as *liquidation bankruptcy.* When considering bankruptcy, most people consult with a bankruptcy attorney, who explains specifically what, in each case, is most likely to be affected.

If you decide not to use an attorney and try instead to use a do-it-yourself bankruptcy kit or guidebook, you must determine to the best of your ability what of your life and property will survive bankruptcy. Consider buying a book on rebuilding your life right at the outset, too, so that you have a good idea of what it takes to start over and get going again on the other side of bankruptcy.

Other than the decision between lawyer and no lawyer, the process for filing Chapter 7 bankruptcy is close to the same for everyone, no matter where in the United States you live. These are the basic steps:

1. You complete a set of forms, provided by the bankruptcy court, listing all your debts and all your property (that is, whatever you own, such as your home, car, furniture, and appliances). Plus, you give detailed information about your income and its sources, your current living expenses, and the money you've spent or given away in the last two years.

You can incur serious penalties for lying to the court or trying to hide assets. Although honest mistakes are not punished, deliberate omissions, misrepresentations, and perjury may be. Your case could be thrown out of court; but prosecution of fraud is on the rise, and lying to the court may even result in a jail sentence.

2. You take the forms, plus the court fee, to the bankruptcy clerk. You cannot pay by personal check, because your credit is no longer viewed as reliable. You must pay cash or with a cashier's check, certified check, or money order.

After you file your forms and pay the fees, you can stop paying on your debts. Also, you may arrange to have wage attachments and payroll deductions for debt repayment stopped at this time. *You may not sell or buy anything, however, without the court's permission.*

3. Your creditors are notified that you have filed for bankruptcy. They are expected to stop calling you for payment, but they have 60 days to file an objection regarding the discharge of any debt that pertains to them.

4. A month or so after you file, you go to the courthouse to meet with the court trustee, who determines what of your property can be turned over to your creditors.

Because neither the state nor the federal government wants you destitute, some items are identified as exempt so that you have the ability to start over. Everything else goes toward your debts.

Exempt items include any equity in your home or car, work tools that you need, furniture, and clothes — although many exempt items are exempt only up to a certain dollar amount.

Even if an item is identified as exempt, you can lose it when you declare bankruptcy if you pledged it as part of a secured debt that had to do with the purchase of the item.

5. The trustee collects and sells all property identified as nonexempt. The money is given to your creditors. Also, all property used as collateral for secured debts returns to your creditors. (If you want to keep it, you must pay for it.)

6. Within a couple of months of your meeting with the trustee, a court hearing takes place. If you completed the necessary steps and have been honest and open with your creditors and the trustee, and if your distress is real, the bankruptcy judge will probably grant you a formal "forgiveness" of dischargeable debts, with the exception of any debt for which a creditor has filed a successful appeal.

7. You begin the process of rebuilding your life, with no credit, little property, and a seriously damaged credit history, and still carrying any nondischargeable debts that are outstanding.

If a judge decides that you have enough income to repay your debts over three to five years, you may be instructed to change your filing from Chapter 7 to Chapter 13.

Chapter 13

Chapter 13 bankruptcy is personal financial reorganization, also known as *wage-earner bankruptcy.*

Not everyone can file Chapter 13. You must be able to repay all, or at least many, of your debts during the three to five years allowed under the plan. (Bear in mind that you don't have to pay interest or finance charges on most of your debts during this period, so your debts will be less than if you repaid them on your own or tried to get a consolidation loan.) In addition, there are limits on how much you can owe in unsecured and secured debt.

As with Chapter 7 bankruptcy, Chapter 13 has its drawbacks. Cosigners of loans have to pay back anything that you can't repay. Chapter 13 goes on your credit record, generally for ten years, although it may be taken off your record after seven years if you have repaid your obligations.

Unlike Chapter 7, Chapter 13 bankruptcy enables you to keep your property. Also, Chapter 13 is less complicated than Chapter 7 bankruptcy, so you're less likely to need an attorney. And you can make up missed payments, such as for auto loans and mortgages, rather than just losing these things to repossession or foreclosure.

Here's how Chapter 13 bankruptcy works:

1. As with Chapter 7, you start the process by filling out forms. You list everything you own and everything you owe. This time, you detail your income and then outline a budget that includes all your necessary living expenses and shows how much money is left over to go toward paying your debts.

2. When you meet with the bankruptcy trustee, he or she asks you questions to make sure that you were being both precise and realistic when designing your budget. The

court wants to make sure that your plan has a good chance of succeeding.

3. If your Chapter 13 bankruptcy plan is accepted, you make monthly payments to the trustee, who deals with your creditors. The court expects you to be faithful in keeping up your end of the bargain and to behave responsibly and honorably. The court also expects you to stay within your budget and will not allow you to spend money on anything that is not, in the court's opinion, essential.

4. As soon as you complete the three to five years of your program, you can begin working on improving your credit record. Some courts have established programs to help you with this rebuilding process.

If, for some reason, it turns out that you cannot repay your debts, you can convert a Chapter 13 into a Chapter 7, but then you face property loss and additional costs. Rebuilding from Chapter 7 bankruptcy is not as easy, so try to avoid letting this happen.

Additional information

Chapter 11 bankruptcy is normally used by struggling businesses. However, some individuals seek this form of bankruptcy if they have exceptionally large debts (in the millions) or own considerable real estate. The filing fees are very high for Chapter 11, and you need a lawyer. (The usual minimum attorney's retainer for a Chapter 11 is $7,500 — this is a major legal battle.)

You have several options if you need more information about this and any other of the various types of bankruptcy, as well as legal information about a wide range of other matters pertaining to credit and debt: Talk to an attorney, visit the library, or access legal advice at sites on the Internet, such as the Self-Help Law Center (go to www.nolo.com and click on Debt & Credit under the Legal Encyclopedia).

If you do decide to use an attorney, using a service like the Self-Help Law Center can prepare you for what's ahead and help you know whether the attorney with whom you're speaking has your best interests in mind.

A variety of resources can help you find a bankruptcy attorney if you decide that you need one:

- You can ask friends or business associates for recommendations.

- The bankruptcy trustees at the court in your area may be able to suggest attorneys who are reliable.

- Your state's bar association more than likely has a referral system.

After you collect recommendations, visit several attorneys to compare prices and determine which ones you feel most comfortable with and with whom you communicate most easily.

Determining Whether Bankruptcy Is for You

Before you go to the trouble and expense of contacting an attorney, appraise your situation and determine if you have anything to gain from filing bankruptcy. Gather your debt worksheets and your budget, and then ask yourself the following questions and think about what your answers might mean when you're considering bankruptcy. Be precise and realistic, because the trustee and judge will be.

- **Do you have any discretionary income left after you make the minimum payments on all bills and cover all essential expenses?**

If your answer is yes, forget bankruptcy. More than likely, the case will be dismissed, and you'll be out the attorney and filing fees.

If your answer is no, go on to the next question.

- **Would a court be likely to view any items in your budget as nonessential?**

If your answer is yes, you have two options: Eliminate the item yourself and put the money toward your bills, or, if the item is important to you, avoid bankruptcy so that you can retain your option of spending that money.

If your answer is no, go on to the next question.

- **Are you behind on payments of secured debts, such as mortgage and car payments?**

If your answer is yes, contact the creditors and try to make arrangements to catch up on payments, as described in Chapter 7, or, if you're on the verge of fore-closure or repossession, you may want to consider filing Chapter 13 bankruptcy.

If your answer is no, continue to pay your bills and budget carefully; you're probably not a good candidate for bankruptcy.

- **Compare all the debts on your debt worksheet to the list of nondischargeable debts earlier in this chapter. Is a considerable portion of your debt nondischargeable?**

If your answer is yes, you have little to gain from filing for bankruptcy.

If your answer is no, go on to the next question.

- **Do you have property that you could sell (that is, without liens or other impediments) that would probably be taken from you if you filed Chapter 7?**

If your answer is yes, you may want to sell it yourself, apply the money toward your bills, and keep your credit record clean.

If your answer is no — that is, either you have no property that could be taken away or there are liens on the property, so it couldn't be sold — bankruptcy may be an option.

- **Did a friend or relative cosign any of the loans that the bankruptcy would affect?**

  If your answer is yes, talk to that individual to find out if he or she is able to repay, because the debt becomes his or hers if you file for bankruptcy. If your friend or relative can repay, perhaps he or she can do so without having you file, and then you can repay him or her in time.

  If your answer is no, continue looking into bankruptcy if you feel that it's necessary.

Pretty much all the other considerations are personal or emotional. Are you comfortable with having the court establish your budget? Are you comfortable with the thought of having this mark against your credit history for ten years and being unable to get loans, credit cards, and so on? Do you lack the discipline to carry out a repayment plan without the threat of legal intervention? Are you willing to give up much of your property to creditors? Will you be able to recover emotionally from the process? This is a serious decision, so make it wisely.

..

CHAPTER 9
CHANGING YOUR LIFESTYLE TO AVOID DEBT

IN THIS CHAPTER

■ Breaking free of "programmed" behaviors

■ Escaping discontent and the urge to spend

■ Redirecting your energies

■ Staying excited about being debt-free

■ Building a financial foundation that helps you succeed

You can go on sheer willpower for only so long. To be really successful for the long term, you have to change the patterns — emotional as well as financial — that helped you get into debt. Rather than being a matter of giving things up, change is a matter of pursuing new things, enriching your life, and avoiding old traps.

As you go through this chapter, you may find that your how-I-got-into-debt worksheet (from Chapter 2) helps you identify areas that need work.

Altering Habits

The mind is an astonishing thing. It captures the ordinary patterns of your life in order to free you up to concentrate on new things. These captured patterns are called *habits*.

Habits are like well-trodden pathways in your brain. Once those pathways are formed, it's hard for electrical impulses to go elsewhere. You've probably experienced this phenomenon. Can you remember a time you were driving somewhere and you made the wrong turn because you usually go that way? That's the result of one of these patterns, called an *entrapment habit.*

Some habits are necessary for survival, but most habits are neither necessary nor helpful. The more of these non-survival habits you can break, the better. Even breaking small habits helps.

The best way to start breaking down little habits is to start with your routines at home. In the morning, as you get ready to start your day, do things in a slightly different order than usual. Put in a different earring first, or put on a different shoe first. This exercise is not as easy as it sounds; you'll probably be surprised at how ingrained even these little habits are.

Your behavior doesn't have to be completely different every day for this exercise to work. In fact, getting through the day would be difficult if you tried to change everything at once. Just try to change one thing each day. Soon, you'll find that your thoughts are less confined. You'll probably find it easier to come up with new ideas or find solutions to problems that stumped you previously.

The flip side of breaking big habits more easily as you change the smaller ones is that if you don't change the smaller ones, the bigger ones are much more difficult to change. The process is sort of like clearing out small rocks and branches so that you can reach the big boulder that is blocking your exit.

As you get better at breaking the little habits, start thinking of the habits you have that involve money. These habits may range from not picking up change that falls on the ground to buying on impulse to overusing credit cards. Here are a few tricks that may help you change your spending habits:

- Don't charge anything under $30. Pay cash or write a check.

- If you see something you want to buy, leave the store. Go somewhere else for a while, or just walk around the block, and ask yourself if you really need the item. Often, as soon as you're away from the store, the impulse will pass.

- If loose change falls on the ground, stop to pick it up (unless your arms are full or you're crossing the street). First, change adds up. Second, contempt for small amounts of money can undermine your intention to take larger amounts of money seriously.

Avoiding Temptation

Avoiding temptation has two sides: The first is to change patterns that put you in the path of temptation. The second is to practice contentment. Combined, these two factors can save you both money and grief.

Stay out of temptation's path

You're bombarded with temptation and have too many easy ways to give in to it. Following are some suggestions that can help you avoid temptation and respond to it when it does hit:

- **Cut up your credit cards.** If you didn't cut them up in Chapter 5, do so now. Keep only the ones that you need for identification, emergencies, or business.

- **Open a charge account.** A *charge account* is one that you have to pay off each month, like American Express. Most credit cards offer *revolving charge accounts* — that is, credit, which means that you can pay over time, and with interest.

- **Use a debit card.** You can't spend more than you currently have in your checking account (although you need to be careful, because you don't want an empty checking account when it comes time to pay bills).

- **Watch videos instead of watching TV (which constantly bombards you with commercials).** Statistics show that, on average, your spending increases by $4 for every hour of TV you watch. If your budget doesn't allow renting videos, remember that the library has them for free.

- **Never just "hang out" in malls.** Avoid even shopping in malls when possible — especially big, fancy malls with lots of stores that you love.

- **Throw out catalogs as soon as they arrive.** Don't browse and ooh and aah over the goodies. Get them out of sight fast.

- **Use coupons, but judiciously.** Coupons can be helpful, but use them only for items you need — don't buy a product just because you have a coupon for it. Also, continue to compare prices; the generic brand or something that's on sale may still be cheaper than the item you have a coupon for. And remember, spending too much time looking for coupons puts your focus on shopping, and that's a focus you're trying to change.

- **Enlist the aid of friends.** Just as you would ask friends not to offer you cake and ice cream if you were on a diet, ask them not to tell you about great sales, new restaurants, or all the stuff they're buying. Ask them to share when they explore inexpensive entertainment options, or invite them to join you in "cheap" entertainment, like picnics or potluck dinners.

Practice contentment

If you're discontented, the least likely reason is that you're living below the poverty line. More likely, you're discontented because you focus on material items, especially the things you don't have. Here are a few steps that can help you reduce the discontentment in your life — and help you build contentment:

- **Cancel magazine subscriptions,** especially if the magazines show you lots of things you don't have or lots of places you haven't gone. Most magazines will refund the amount you paid for any undelivered issues, which gives you a bit of handy cash. The more important result, however, is that you are not constantly dissatisfied.

- **Explore places that are free or that you can get into for a very small fee.** These places might include forest preserves, botanical gardens, beaches, parks, local free concerts, libraries, and museums. Delight in the fact that someone's foresight or thoughtfulness made these activities available, as well as that they can enrich your life more than some costlier pleasures can.

- **Count your blessings.** Think about all that you *do* have, whether it's stuff (a home, a mode of transportation, a pair of shoes, some flowers in a pot by the window), people (family, friends, a support network), or your health.

- **Don't indulge in "magic thinking."** This is the tendency to dream of something (primarily money) coming along and making all your problems go away. You've already indulged in magic thinking if you've ever purchased a lottery ticket. Aside from the astronomical odds against your winning, this behavior is self-defeating. You're looking for a "fairy godmother" to come along and solve your problems. Even winning doesn't solve problems if your behavior remains the same. (And remember, $1 per day can save you $27,000 in interest on your mortgage.)

- **Focus on people more than on stuff.** Material things aren't really the key to happiness; they're merely props on the stage of life. Some "plays" are more complex than others and require more props — but more complicated doesn't mean better. The element that makes the "stories" work is the characters — the people.

- **Choose to be content.** Psychologists have shown that often, people feel what they have *decided* to feel. So decide to be happy with what you have. Decide to focus on the partner or children you have. Decide to be delighted with the beauty of a sunrise and the wonder of the changing seasons. Decide to be contented.

Don't mistake contentment for resignation. You can be happy and continue to improve your life. A wise person once said, "The grass is greener where you water it."

Finding New Interests

So you're avoiding temptation and practicing contentment. But what do you do for fun? Actually, an amazingly wide array of entertainment, adventures, and knowledge is available. I mentioned some in preceding sections: museums, gardens, forest preserves, and other delights. Find them and enjoy them.

Hobbies are also a great way to entertain yourself at a low cost. (Shopping doesn't count!) Consider these general categories of hobbies:

- **Studying:** Finding out about history, science, or art can make you a more interesting person and add richness and depth to your life.

- **Skills:** Becoming proficient in skills like carpentry and electrical work can save you money by enabling you to do minor repairs around the house yourself.

■ **Arts and crafts:** Developing your artistic side can be fulfilling. These hobbies also offer you money savings in the form of making gifts rather than buying them.

Local continuing-education programs usually have low-priced programs with enough variety to interest almost anyone. Offerings can include anything from gardening to martial arts to investing.

Your local library is a great resource for information about all sorts of organizations and opportunities in your area, including concerts, discussion groups, and classes. The library may even offer programs on-site, including lectures, movies, and demonstrations.

Getting Beyond Yourself

If your debt was not caused by circumstances beyond your control, it's probably at least partially due to a focus on *self*. Running up thousands of dollars on your credit cards is hard to do if your focus is on the needs of others.

Learning to be contented with what you have is an important part of getting out of this trap. Another part — something that actually contributes to your sense of contentment — is getting involved in the lives of others. I'm not talking about the lives of people who can help you, but the lives of those from whom you have nothing to gain.

Here are some ways to get beyond yourself and get involved with others. Not only are you changing your focus, but you're also helping to change your world.

■ If you belong to an organization of some sort, get on a committee, help with the newsletter, or teach a class.

■ Get to know your neighbors.

- Help the less fortunate by volunteering. Homeless shelters and soup kitchens are always looking for volunteers. Suicide hotlines and crisis pregnancy centers are always short-handed. Find out what services are provided in your community and see if you can help. (Call the local United Way office if you can't think of any services.)

- Tutor in an adult literacy program.

Don't do something because it is high profile and gets you acclaim; do it because it helps people. The idea is to pay attention to the people around you, to enrich your life by letting them in, to increase your contentment by noticing their difficulties, and to give more than you get.

Thinking Long-Term

Because your recovery from debt may take a while, you need to think big-picture and long-term. Really improving your life — not just your financial situation, but your whole life — may involve bigger changes than you'd previously considered, and sometimes you need something to smack you in the face before you realize that change is desirable. The following sections describe some situations that you may want to think about and the changes that could improve them.

This list is not exhaustive. As you continue your journey, you may think of other things that need to change that are not necessarily obviously connected to debt, whether they're triggers for emotion-based spending or circumstances that increase your costs. But don't be afraid to consider bigger changes if they'll improve your life and make getting out of debt easier.

Pursue further education

If further education could have a positive effect on your income, pursue it. There's generally a strong correlation between knowing more and earning more, so work to gain knowledge — whether it's a GED or an MBA, a new computer language or certification in an additional area of auto maintenance, a professional enrichment course or formal education, knowledge or skills.

If you don't know what specific courses would improve your current situation or advance you to another, check with your employer. Ask what they would value, what they would be willing to pay more to get. And find out if your employer offers reimbursement for tuition or pays for classes that improve your skills.

Look into local continuing-education programs, offerings by professional organizations, online universities, community colleges, and other educational options. Because a lot of people are currently juggling both jobs and education, there are lots of alternatives to the traditional routes to learning.

Change jobs or careers

If you overspend in part to relieve the stress that you build up in an unacceptable job situation, consider changing jobs. This is not a short-term solution or one to be taken lightly, but it's worth considering. Here are some steps you could take — even if you're just trying to decide if a change is a good idea.

■ Create a list of all the things you like and don't like about your job. Analyze the list, asking yourself if the things you don't like are things that you may be able to change, if the things you do like are unique to the job or available elsewhere, and if you can improve your situation by changing jobs.

■ Search out organizations from which you can learn about new jobs, such as local networking groups, professional organizations, and entrepreneurs' groups — check the business section of a local paper for ideas and contacts.

■ Start scanning the help-wanted ads, either in your local newspaper or on an Internet service such as www.headhunter.net or www.monster.com.

■ Update your résumé so that you'll be ready in case something catches your eye.

A career change is more significant than a job change, but if you're not satisfied by what you're doing now, a change may be what you need. Before you start, however, consider the following:

■ If the career change would involve a cut in pay, use this time as an opportunity to study and plan, because pursuing something at a lower pay level is not in your best interest until you're out of debt.

■ If your desired career would leave you at the same pay level or improve your pay, this is a good time to focus on studying, planning, and moving toward the new career.

■ If you have a longtime dream, start working toward it part-time, in addition to your regular job. If doing so creates additional income, that's even better, but it's not necessary. The point is to move toward a better life both financially and emotionally. Having a positive goal that excites you makes other goals easier to pursue.

■ If you're dissatisfied with what you're doing but you don't have a specific idea about what you want to pursue, investigate options. Take a few courses. Talk to friends. Consult a career counselor.

Relocate

Think carefully about your feelings for the place you're living — not the house, but the surroundings. Don't confuse your dislike for your job or financial situation with a dislike for where you live, and don't mistake discontentment with a modest lifestyle for feeling like you belong elsewhere. This is not about upgrading your lifestyle; it's about finding a place that's both more soothing and more affordable. And don't move without carefully considering the costs, because you don't want to increase your debt burden.

Here are some questions to ask yourself, plus some considerations and sources of information to help you come to a decision:

- Would you be happier in a different setting — city versus suburbs, small town versus big town?

- Are prices too high where you live? Is there somewhere else where you would enjoy living and where the cost of living is lower, but where you can still obtain a reasonable income?

- Are you far away from family and friends, necessitating lots of travel and expensive phone bills to stay in touch?

- Analyze your feelings honestly. Discuss them with friends and family. Do nothing in a hurry. Be open with others and with yourself. Ask yourself whether you really feel like you don't belong or are just trying to escape your debt, your job, your responsibilities, or yourself.

- Check the library or bookstore for guides to places that might interest you. A number of available books list statistics such as cost of living, average wages, housing costs, weather, schools, and recreational opportunities for places all around the United States.

Keeping Your Goals Fresh

If nothing ever changed, you wouldn't need to worry about this step. But everything changes — you, your life, the world. Change affects your goals in two ways: First, it makes your circumstances different, so your original goals may not be completely accurate anymore. Second, it can keep you so busy that you forget about your goals.

For both reasons, you need to review your goals on a regular basis (about every six months). Reviews give you an opportunity to check your progress and incorporate any new information into your goals. The following sections outline some steps that can help you stay on track and keep your goals in sight.

Update

■ Continue to keep your budget worksheet current, not only filling in the "actual" column each month but also redoing any sections that change, such as increase in income or differences in expenses.

■ Update any notes or signs that you've created to remind yourself of your goals. For example, if you have a sign on the bathroom mirror saying that you're 5 years away from debt-free living, create a new sign when you're 4½ years away, 4 years away, and so on.

■ If you're charting your progress in any way, make sure to keep the chart current.

Restate

■ Create new goals if old ones become obsolete.

■ Frame your goals in different terms to make them fit more precisely with your changing circumstances. For example, your goals may include new elements, such as a career change, continuing your education, or having children.

■ Recommit yourself to achieving your goals.

Celebrate

■ Every time you achieve a goal, whether it's paying off a credit card, successfully renegotiating your mortgage, or seeing the end of your car payments, celebrate.

■ Think of ways to celebrate that cost little or no money, such as a potluck dinner (the expense is shared), going out for an ice cream cone, or spending a day at a park.

■ Share the good news with anyone who knows what you're going through, whether it's a few friends or a large support group. Enjoy the congratulations.

■ Congratulate yourself. Put up a sign where you can see it that reminds you of the goals you have achieved. Remember how effective those gold stars were when you were a kid? They may still work.

Finding Support

Remember

Regardless of the cause of your debt, having support makes getting out of debt easier. If you've addressed larger issues and sought healing through a recovery program of some sort, you may have found much support. But even if there's nothing from which you need to recover (other than your money woes), bringing a friend along on the trip helps. Here are some of the reasons:

■ Having someone to sympathize or encourage not only is satisfying, but also can save your recovery. No burden is so light that it isn't even lighter with two people carrying it.

■ Having someone know what you're doing can keep you on track.

- You need to have someone to help you celebrate your successes.

- Always having to say "no" when people call and ask you to do things that cost money gets tiring. If you have friends who know what you're going through, they'll call with ideas that are within your budget. Friends may be willing to help in other useful ways, like lending you books and videos, letting you borrow their tools, and exchanging services (lawn mowing for baby-sitting, painting for tutoring, and so on).

Remember

Having someone know that you're going through recovery can be the difference between success and failure. Find a friend with whom you can share, or someone in a position you respect (teacher, minister, rabbi, counselor) with whom you can talk, so that someone else knows what you're doing. Often, even if you lose sight of your goal, you'll stay on course to avoid disappointing that person.

Working toward a More Secure Future

One of the best things you can do, intellectually and psychologically, is to focus on the very real possibility of having a financially secure future. Not only does this help you get through the debt recovery process by offering you a positive goal, but it also helps ensure that you stay out of debt.

Pursuing information

A habit of pursuing information can prepare you both for the future that you can imagine now and for any changes that might alter that vision. Throughout the debt recovery process, you can build your financial knowledge, and afterward you can continue to gain knowledge and experience as you begin to build financial security.

You want to find out about things that can help you meet your changing goals. Here are some ideas for what to study when:

- While you're still on the troubled side of your goal, pursue information about improving your debt profile or rebuilding your credit rating.

- As you approach your goal, begin picking up information about savings options. Find out what kinds of savings programs your bank offers. Find out how much money you need to open a money market account and what minimum balance you need for a no-charge savings account.

Once you reach your goal, continue to add to your knowledge of financial concepts, savings options, and investing.

Most libraries have a wide range of books and magazines on finance and economics. (Even if you're ready to subscribe to a financial magazine, reading them first at the library enables you to decide ahead of time which one you like best.) See the CliffsNotes Resource Center at the end of this book for suggestions of books to consider.

Starting to save

As soon as you have *any* discretionary income left after paying your bills, start saving. It doesn't have to be a lot — at least not at first — but you should put something in savings on a consistent basis.

You need to create several categories of savings, each important for different reasons:

- First, start your emergency fund. You should have enough money set aside to cover three to six months of expenses. You need this money to be in a relatively liquid account, so a savings account or money market account of some sort is probably your best bet. If you've been gathering information, you should know where you want to put your money by the time you have some to save.

Take the concept of an emergency fund seriously. Even if it takes you a while to build up the fund, keep working on it. Never use the emergency fund for a nonessential expense. Protecting this account is an important part of protecting yourself from the risk of future debt problems.

■ If your employer offers a retirement program, find out what's involved. If it's a 401(k) or profit-sharing arrangement, contribute something to the account. If no program is offered, check with your bank or tax accountant about setting up an IRA. The earlier you start a retirement fund, whether on your own or through an employer, the easier it is to establish a substantial retirement nest egg.

■ After you establish an emergency fund and begin putting aside money for retirement, you'll probably want to start a general fund. You can use this fund for buying items for which you might once have relied on credit or installment plans (appliances, furniture, or a new car). The money can go toward the down payment on a new house or a child's (or your own) education.

■ As you get more comfortably situated, you may want to consider investing in stocks or mutual funds. (However, you don't want to invest until you have your emergency fund in place and are contributing to your retirement fund.) Investing is a great way to build wealth, but it should *not* be your first line of savings.

So pursue knowledge, save your money, and consider investing. You may end up so far away from debt that you can hardly remember it. But do remember it a little, if only to help you stay out of trouble, and perhaps to help others by sharing what you've learned.

CLIFFSNOTES REVIEW

Use this CliffsNotes Review to practice what you've learned in this book and to build your confidence in doing the job right the first time. After you work through the review questions, the problem-solving exercises, and the fun and useful practice projects, you're well on your way to achieving your goal of getting out of debt.

Q&A

1. If you have $1,500 on a credit card with a 21 percent interest rate, about how long will it take you to pay off the balance if you always make the minimum payment (assuming that you make no more charges on the card)?

   a. 5 years

   b. 7 years

   c. 10 years

   d. 14 years

2. True or False: Using a consolidator does not get noted on your credit record.

3. Loans for which you must put up collateral are called _____ loans.

4. These debts are not discharged (that is, they are not erased) when you declare bankruptcy.

   a. Student loans

   b. Alimony or child support

   c. Taxes

   d. All of the above

5. A budget needs to be

   a. Rigid and static

   b. Realistic and flexible

   c. Easy and informal

6. What are the three keys to keeping your budget up-to-date?

1) _____

2) _____

3) _____

7. What is considered the maximum recommended percentage of take-home pay going to your debt obligations?

a. 15 percent

b. 20 percent

c. 25 percent

d. 35 percent

8. Name two reasons that Chapter 13 bankruptcy is better than Chapter 7 bankruptcy.

1) _____

2) _____

9. The Fair Debt Collection Practices Act protects you from

a. Abusive practices by collection agencies

b. Anyone to whom you owe money

c. Paying interest on debts

10. When you're at a point where you can start saving, what are the three primary funds that you want to make sure you have in place?

1) _____

2) _____

3) _____

Answers: 1. d. 2. False. 3. Secured. 4. d. 5. b. 6. Regularity, accuracy, honesty. 7. c. 8. With Chapter 13, you don't lose your property, and it doesn't remain on your credit report as long. 9. a. 10. Emergency fund, retirement fund, and general fund.

Scenarios

1. Someone telephones you at home and starts to tell you about an amazing offer. It won't be available for long, so you have to buy it now or miss this opportunity. What should you do?

_____

2. You receive an offer in the mail for a credit card. It sounds like a great offer, but you see no information about interest rates or grace periods. You should _____

_____.

3. People at work have a football pool, and all employees are asked to chip in $10 a week. You should _____

_____.

Answers: 1. If it's something that interests you, ask for printed information to be mailed to you. If they refuse, say, "Thank you, I'm not interested," and then immediately hang up. 2. Throw it out. Credit card companies must, by law, supply this information, so the offer must be a fraud. 3. Be honest and say, "Sorry, I'm broke."

Consider This

■ Did you know that paying just a little bit over the minimum payment can make a major difference in how fast you pay off your credit cards? See Chapter 5 to find out how much of a difference even $5 a month makes.

■ Did you know that a consolidator does _not_ offer you an easy way out of debt? In Chapter 8, you can find out the potential pitfalls of consolidations, plus get information on when they might be a good choice for you.

■ Did you know that involving others in your recovery process is vital to your success? In Chapters 4 and 10, you can review the reasons and find tips.

CLIFFSNOTES RESOURCE CENTER

The learning doesn't need to stop here. CliffsNotes Resource Center shows you the best of the best — links to the best information in print and online about debt, money management, and other financial topics. Look for these terrific resources at the library, at your favorite bookstore, and on the Internet. While you're online, make your first stop www.cliffsnotes.com, because we've put together an even bigger CliffsNotes Resource Center there.

Books

This CliffsNotes book is one of many great books about getting out of debt published by IDG Books Worldwide, Inc., and other publishers. If you want some great next-step books, check out these other publications:

CliffsNotes Investing for the First Time, by Tracey Longo. Once you've paid off your debts, this book shows you how to "spend" your money wisely — by putting it investments that make your money grow. IDG Books Worldwide, Inc., $8.99.

Home Buying For Dummies, by Eric Tyson and Ray Brown. When you achieve enough financial independence that you can begin to think about purchasing a house, this book walks you through the entire process and helps you get the best deal possible on the house of your dreams. IDG Books Worldwide, Inc., $16.99.

Success For Dummies, by Zig Ziglar. Getting out of debt is a big part of your financial success. To get the rest of your life on the right path, look to this book by famed motivational speaker Zig Ziglar. IDG Books Worldwide, Inc., $19.99.

Changing for Good: A revolutionary, six-stage program for overcoming bad habits and moving your life positively forward, by James O. Prochaska, Ph.D., John C. Norcross, Ph.D., and Carlo C. DiClemente, Ph.D. This book explains the psychology of change and then guides you through preparing to change, taking action, maintaining success, and recovering from relapses. Applies to any self-defeating behaviors, not just money. Avon Books, $12.50.

Financial Peace: Restoring Financial Hope to You and Your Family, by David Ramsey and Sharon Ramsey. Guide to rebuilding your life, credit history, and finances after suffering bankruptcy. Penguin Books, $22.95.

You can find these books in your favorite bookstores (on the Internet and at stores near you). We also have three Web sites that you can use to read about all the books we publish:

- **www.cliffsnotes.com**
- **www.dummies.com**
- **www.idgbooks.com**

Internet

The Internet is another great source of additional information. Check out these sites, for example:

CNN Financial Network, cnnfn.com — Good for becoming more knowledgeable about the world of money. Serious news on the world of finance.

The Motley Fool, www.fool.com — A fun, user-friendly finance/investing site that states as its goal, "To Educate, Amuse, Enrich." Includes information on how to invest, discussion groups, stock tips, and a free e-mail investment letter.

Joy of Simple Living, www.JoyofSimpleLiving.com — The companion site to the book *The Joy of Simple Living*, by Jeff Davidson. The goal of the book and Web site is to help you make your life easier and more contented, at home and at work, by uncluttering your life and living within your means. The site offers valuable links to Breathing Space Resource Center and Simple Living Network.

Smart Money Magazine Online, www.smartmoney. com — *The Wall Street Journal*'s magazine of personal business and finance offers news, discussion forums, and a range of tools, including Your Portfolio and Investor Calendar.

USA Today Money section, www.usatoday.com/money/ mfront.htm — Readable news in the familiar format of *USA Today*. The site offers investor tools, top news stories related to money, updates on the stock market, resources, and more.

Send Us Your Favorite Tips

In your quest for learning, have you ever experienced that sublime moment when you figure out a trick that saves time or trouble? Perhaps you realized you were taking ten steps to accomplish something that could have taken two. Or you found a little-known workaround that gets great results. If you've discovered a useful tip that helped you get out of debt and you'd like to share it, the CliffsNotes staff would love to hear from you. Go to our Web site at www.cliffsnotes.com and click the Talk to Us button. If we select your tip, we may publish it as part of CliffsNotes Daily, our exciting, free e-mail newsletter. To find out more or to subscribe to a newsletter, go to www.cliffsnotes.com on the Web.

INDEX

NUMBERS AND SYMBOLS

COMING SOON FROM CLIFFSNOTES

Online Shopping

HTML

Choosing a PC

Beginning Programming

Careers

Windows 98 Home Networking

eBay Online Auctions

PC Upgrade and Repair

Business

Microsoft Word 2000

Microsoft PowerPoint 2000

Finance

Microsoft Outlook 2000

Digital Photography

Palm Computing

Investing

Windows 2000

Online Research

COMING SOON FROM CLIFFSNOTES
Buying and Selling on eBay

Have you ever experienced the thrill of finding an incredible bargain at a specialty store or been amazed at what people are willing to pay for things that you might toss in the garbage? If so, then you'll want to learn about eBay — the hottest auction site on the Internet. And CliffsNotes *Buying and Selling on eBay* is the shortest distance to eBay proficiency. You'll learn how to:

■ Find what you're looking for, from antique toys to classic cars

■ Watch the auctions strategically and place bids at the right time

■ Sell items online at the eBay site

■ Make the items you sell attractive to prospective bidders

■ Protect yourself from fraud

Here's an example of how the step-by-step CliffsNotes learning process simplifies placing a bid at eBay:

1. Scroll to the Web page form that is located at the bottom of the page on which the auction item itself is presented.

2. Enter your registered eBay username and password and enter the amount you want to bid. A Web page appears that lets you review your bid before you actually submit it to eBay. After you're satisfied with your bid, click the Place Bid button.

3. Click the Back button on your browser until you return to the auction listing page. Then choose⇨Reload (Netscape Navigator) or View⇨Refresh (Microsoft Internet Explorer) to reload the Web page information. Your new high bid appears on the Web page, and your name appears as the high bidder.